Stephen W. King

San Diego State University

Communication and Social Influence

Addison-Wesley Publishing Company

Reading, Massachusetts • Menlo Park, California
London • Amsterdam • Don Mills, Ontario • Sydney

This book is in the
ADDISON-WESLEY SERIES IN HUMAN COMMUNICATION

Consulting Editor
C. David Mortensen

*To the
memory of
my father*

Foreword

Society is often described as an ongoing system of communication maintained by persons committed to the principle of consistent action. Similarly, this series in Human Communication is designed to explore the ongoing and pervasive impact of communication on the actions and patterns of everyday experience. The series provides a flexible and integrated discussion of key concepts, problems, topics, and issues related to "person-centered" subject matter. The books strive to be readable, non-technical, and broadly based without sacrificing the depth needed to challenge serious students.

In developing such an important collection of texts, Addison-Wesley has called upon a well-known group of teachers whose competence is ideally suited to their texts. *Communication Inquiry: A Perspective on a Process* by Gerald R. Miller and Henry E. Nicholson introduces students to various ways of studying communicative behavior as an integral dimension of personal and social experience. *Dyadic Communication: A Transactional Perspective* by William Wilmot focuses on the complex and fascinating processes that shape the experience of communication in interpersonal social situations. *Communication and Social Influence* by Stephen W. King broadens the study of communication to the context of what is known about the potentials and hazards of using language to influence and persuade others. An overview of language and speech as communication codes, within and between individuals, is the subject of Larry Wilder's *Speech, Language, and Communication* (forthcoming). The larger theoretical aspects of human communication are examined in *Analoguing: Theory and Model Consutuction in Communication* by Leonard C. Hawes and in

Perspectives on Communication Theory by Jesse G. Delia (forthcoming). *Analoguing* provides the first systematic treatment of the requirements of developing theories about the underlying nature of communicative experience. Delia's text will complement other books in the series by providing a broadly based synthesis of recent contributions to the study of communication theory.

These brief, integrated paperback texts are suitable for a wide range of purposes and courses within communication and the social sciences. Used in combination or alone with other texts and supplements, they will enhance and enrich the study of human communication.

August 1974   C. David Mortensen

Preface

This book was written to provide students, and perhaps scholars, with a useful conceptualization and analysis of data pertaining to a very ill-defined but significant sphere of human behavior—"social influence." Previous writings that have included chapters or sections on social influence have done so under a wide and diverse variety of topics—"cultural change," "psychology of the poor," "persuasion," "societal change," "conformity," and "conflict resolution." Although all of these writings, plus the theory and research in the field, were examined in the preparation of this book, the view of social influence taken here will be broader than that of persuasion, but narrower than that of all forms of social or societal change. The specific focus of this study is the theory and research that pertains directly to the phenomenon of social change as it is manifested in the influence of one or more person's behavior on one or more other persons.

Treatment of social influence in this book reflects certain basic principles. The first of these is a commitment to what is called the "process" notion of human behavior. To emphasize the "ongoingness" of social influence, the main divisions of the book relate to different kinds of influence processes—informational and normative. Another principle reflected in this volume is my bias that insofar as possible, it should be based on the findings of experimental research. This experimental bias resulted in two problems. First, experimentation is continually being conducted in all of the areas of research with which this book is concerned. Therefore, this book can be no more than a statement of where we are today. It is definitely not a "final answer"; it may not even provide any answer in some areas, as research into some problem areas has only been begun. Second, there are many ongoing debates about such issues as which theory best explains a given behavior or which variables account for certain phenomena. Where the data were sufficient to allow conclusions, conclusions were drawn. Where the data were still too skimpy to justify conclusions, no answer was attempted.

Thus, to answer the traditional question as to why this book was written, I hope the book itself is sufficient reply. (Of course, it isn't, so I will attempt some introspection here.) In addition to trying to summarize the current state of knowledge in social influence and to reflect my fascination with the process attributes of this very important phenomenon, this book was written with an eye toward classroom use. Accordingly, theoretic minutiae and extended debates of methodology, the grist of the academician's mill, were excluded. In their stead, examples of social influence involving semifictitious characters were liberally employed.

Naturally, the writing of this book, being a process itself, had many important influences, and I would like to recognize the importance of these influences here. My thinking about social influence was significantly affected by several friends and scholars. Specifically, I owe important intellectual debts to Walt Fisher, Gerald Miller, Norman Miller, Dave Mortensen, and Kenneth Sereno. Several individuals read all or part of this manuscript, improved my thinking on numerous substantive issues, and assisted in the resolution of difficult writing problems: Walt Fisher, Dave Mortensen, Herb Simons, Al Weitzel, and Bill Wilmot. Finally, my wife, Leatha-Ann, deserves special appreciation for not only typing the entire manuscript too many times to recount, but also for her boundless patience with an often moody husband-writer.

San Diego, California   S. W. K.
December 1973

Contents

Chapter One

A Frame of Reference

Man is a social animal. The seeming triviality of this statement is overshadowed by the importance of its consequences. Two consequences of man's social nature are communication and social influence. As a result of man's being a social animal, he communicates with and influences others in a wide variety of circumstances and by numerous means, as the following examples illustrate.

- In 1897 a psychologist and amateur bicycle-racing enthusiast named Triplett observed that bicycle racers performed better when competing head-to-head than when racing the clock. Triplett was intrigued by the obvious fact that the performance of one individual was altered by the presence of another. Triplett's observation of this social phenomenon was more important than his explanation for it; but for historical interest, it is noted that Triplett proposed the theory of "dynamogenesis." His theory contended that the improved performance was due to the "competitive instinct" aroused by the presence of another rider.

- LeBon (1896) studied another important social phenomenon—crowd behavior. He noted that people in mobs apparently do things they never would do by themselves. "What was it about a mob," asked LeBon, "that so altered those in it that they would commit such heinous acts as murder?" His explanation of this phenomenon was naive (man loses his rational abilities and is susceptible to emotional appeals as if in a hypnotic trance), but the recognition of the importance of this social behavior was critical.

You will probably be able to sympathize with the person in the next example of social influence. His experience is a very common one.*

- Clyde, a hypothetical college sophomore taking Psychology 1, was required to participate in ten hours of exper-

---

*This technique for demonstrating the effect of a group on an individual was first developed by Asch. See S. E. Asch, "Effects of Group Pressure upon the Modification and Distortion of Judgments," in H. Guetzkow, ed., *Groups, Leadership and Men*, Pittsburgh: Carnegie Press, 1951, pp. 177–190.

imentation to get a good grade. One Monday morning he was told to report to the room next to the cockroach lab in the basement of the Psychology building. He and four other students were led into the lab and seated in a row in front of a projection screen. A strange-looking researcher told them, "This is going to be a test of your perceptual ability. We are going to present three lines on the screen with a letter under each one. Also, you will see a line with a number under it. We want you to match the numbered line with the lettered line of the same length." The first set of lines was presented.

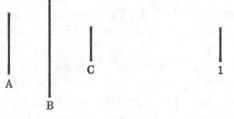

The first student said "C." So did the second, third, and fourth students, who, unbeknownst to Clyde, were being paid five dollars to say what the experimenter wanted them to say.

Clyde said "C" and thought, "How stupid, I should have taken the Psychology of Sexual Deviance: An Introductory Survey." The second set of lines was presented.

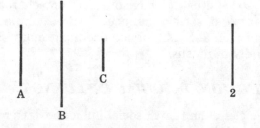

The first person said "C." Clyde laughed, he knew it was "A."

The second person said "C." Clyde frowned.

The third and fourth persons said "C." Clyde regretted ever having considered Psychology as a major.

Clyde's turn to report. He said, "Er—huh—uh—(gulp) —ah—let me see now—er—C!"

• Doob and Gross (1968) had a confederate drive either a 1966 Chrysler Crown Imperial (a high-status car) or a rusty 1954 Ford station wagon (a low-status car) to a particular stoplight. When the light turned green, the driver just sat there. The researchers observed the behavior of the people in the cars immediately behind the stopped cars. Eighteen of 36 people behind the high-status car didn't honk their horns, whereas only 6 of 38 people behind the low-status car didn't. Conversely, 18 people honked twice at the low-status car, and only 7 people honked twice at the high-status car.

• On March 27, 1964 the following story appeared in the *New York Times* reporting the murder of Kitty Genovese:

> For more than half an hour 38 respectable, law-abiding citizens in Queens, watched a killer stalk and stab a woman in three separate attacks in Kew Gardens. Twice the sound of their voices and the sudden glow of their bedroom lights interrupted him and frightened him off. Each time he returned, sought her out, and stabbed her again. Not one person telephoned the police during the assault; one witness called after the woman was dead.

Though it may not be immediately obvious, these vastly different social situations have one common characteristic: each is an example of social influence. These examples illustrate an important fact: Social influence occurs in many situations and by a variety of means.

A DEFINITION OF SOCIAL INFLUENCE

To arrive at a definition of social influence, let's reconsider the examples just discussed. In each case an individual or collection of individuals affected another individual or collection of individuals in some manner: the presence of one bicycle rider apparently prompted another to ride faster than he had alone; mobs seemingly affected people in a manner which caused them to do things they never would normally even consider; Clyde yielded to group pressure; drivers of high-status cars were treated more courteously than were drivers of low-status cars; and the number of bystanders affected each bystander's perception of individual responsibility in an emergency situation. In every case there was an apparent change in thought or behavior. Is *change* the essence of social influence?

The notion of change may well be the key to the concept of social influence. March (1955), for example, explained social influence as a deviation or change from predicted behavior. Specifically, he argued that if everything about human behavior were known, we could predict for any given individual within a particular environment the "path of behavior" he would follow. Therefore, he concluded, "it is in harmony with the more frequent uses of the term 'influence' and with the present sense of that term to say that if the individual *deviates* from the predicted path of behavior, influence has occurred, and specifically that it is influence which has induced the change" (pp. 434–435). Thus, influence can be said to have occurred whenever an individual's behavior deviates from that predicted on the basis of some temporally prior set of conditions.

Each example covered earlier could be subsumed by this concept of influence. For example, if one predicted the riding speed of a given bicycle racer on the basis of his solo performance and then observed the inaccuracy of that prediction when the racer raced head-to-head with another bicyclist, the change in behavior or deviation from expectation would be a sign of the existence of social influence. Indeed, in every example mentioned earlier the behavior investigated drew interest because it deviated from reasonable expectation.

But not all deviation from expected behavior can be attributed to social influence. If a person leaves on a trip from point A to point B, it would be reasonable to predict or expect that he would arrive at point B. If, however, on the way the traveler encountered a washed-out bridge and was forced to go to point C, a deviation or change from expected behavior, influence may have occurred, but not social influence. *Social influence is change or deviation from expectation that results from other people's behavior.* Thus, for the purposes of this book, social influence is defined as the *process by which the behavior of an individual or collection of individuals induces change in the state of another individual or collection of individuals.* It is social influence when a political candidate's campaign literature persuades you to vote for him. It is social influence when a child imitates his parents (e.g., four out of five people who smoke have parents who smoked). It is social influence when your liberal political science professor's lectures result in your registering as a Democrat. It is social influence if this book induces you to believe that social influence is a significant attribute of human behavior and a pervasive phenomenon in our society.

SOCIAL INFLUENCE AND RELATED CONCEPTS

Social influence is obviously an important aspect of the social environment. As such, it is inevitably related to a variety of other social processes. Two of the most easily recognizable and important processes related to social influence are causation and power.

Causation

At first glance, social influence and causality might appear identical. Although social influence and causality are both relational constructs, social-influence relations are distinct from causal relations on two counts. First, to assert that A caused B is to assert more than that A influenced B. Social influence admits the possibility of many sources of influence, of which one is A, whereas the notion of causality asserts that A is the *only* cause of B. Causal relations are more restrictive than are influence relations. Second, causation is strictly unidirectional, or asymmetrical, whereas the concept of social influence allows for mutual, or reciprocal, influence.

An example may clarify these distinctions. If you were deeply impressed by a political candidate's speech and ultimately voted for him, the speech probably influenced your decision, but it was probably not the sole cause of your vote.

Surely you would have used other information in arriving at your decision, such as the opinions of family and friends and your own prior knowledge. In short, there was more than one cause of your behavior. Additionally, your approval of the speech, manifested by hearty clapping at the conclusion, probably influenced the candidate's perception of how his campaign was going. Thus, there was reciprocal influence.

Power

Social influence and power ought to be distinguished. Although many theorists, such as Lewin (1951), treat them as synonymous concepts, most agree that "the concept of power has the conceptual property of *potentiality*" (Blau, 1964, p. 152). That is, power is the potential for influence, and influence is the result of actualized power. For example, a sergeant has power over a private, but he may or may not use it. When he does, he influences the private; he does not "power" him.

SOCIAL INFLUENCE AND COMMUNICATION

Communication and social influence are intimately interrelated. One researcher concluded, for example, that "to study influence one must first study communication. For influence cannot occur without some form of communication" (Walter, 1963, p. 24). Similarly, "if one theme underlies all systems of communication, it is social influence" (Mortensen, 1972, p. 357). But just as the concepts of "love," "democracy," and "honorable peace," are easy to discuss at cocktail parties and in introductions to books but are often difficult to apply to reality, the concept of "communication" must be defined if its relationship to social influence is to be explored.

A Definition of Communication

Rather than survey all the definitions that have been proposed and try to select one from this definition delicatessen, we will stipulate a definition of communication that identifies the conditions necessary for an act of communication to be said to have occurred. That is, communication will be characterized rather than defined in the strictest sense.

The most fundamental characteristic of communication is *the assignation of meaning to behavior.* Communication, therefore, can be said to have occurred whenever one individual perceives another's behavior and attaches significance or meaning to his perception. Communication has occurred when you see another person direct an obscene gesture your way. Communication has occurred when for six consecutive years you don't receive a Christmas card from a "friend." Communication has occurred when someone laughs at a joke you told. The next section will explore the points of similarity between social influence and communication.

Characteristics of Social Influence and Communication

Social influence and communication are both characterized by a number of fundamental attributes. Indeed, these processes share many of the same characteristics. Both processes are transactional in nature, both are inevitable results of social situations, both are receiver phenomena, and both are context-bound. Recognizing the importance of these shared characteristics is crucial to your understanding of social influence and communication.

Both Are Transactional Processes. A process point of view argues that neither social influence nor communication "has *a* beginning, *an* end, a fixed sequence of events. It is not static, at rest. It is moving. The ingredients within the process interact; each affects all the others" (Berlo, 1960, p. 24). The idea of process "*implies a continuous interaction of an indefinitely large number of variables with a concomitant, continuous change in the values taken by these variables*" (Miller, 1966, p. 33). If one attempts to examine a single element of a process (e.g., the organization of a message or the structure of a group exercising social influence), the isolation of that element distorts the nature of the on-going process and limits the information available about the element because it is out of its natural, changing environment. Most complex social phenomena are processes. The attraction you feel for your best friend, for example, cannot be analyzed in temporally discrete terms—it was, is, and will be continually evolving. It cannot even be asserted that your feeling "began" when you met the person, because the psychological frame of reference you use in evaluating people was the result of much prior experience.

All processes are difficult to explain. The necessary linearity of language usage (one word after another) virtually precludes accurate description of a process. Furthermore, in a real sense, process cannot be scientifically observed. That is, observation is necessarily limited to temporally successive observations (one can only observe aspects of the environment serially), thus severely restricting the study of events of process. Not only is the discussion and observation of process difficult, theorizing about a process is limited, for the most part, to focusing attention on an equilibrium state (Coleman, 1963, p. 68). That is, since it is virtually impossible to describe an on-going process, theory must "stop" the process to describe it. But just as the impossibility of achieving absolute zero has not substantially slowed the advance of physics, the process nature of communication and social influence does not preclude discussion, research, and theorizing about these processes. However, in the study of social influence and communication, those attempts at description, research, and theorizing that incorporate the process notion are the most fruitful.

Given this description of process, it is evident that both social influence and communication are processes. Both communication and social influence defy linear description. What is stimulus and what is response, who is sender and who is receiver, and what is cause and what is effect—all are judgments based on an arbitrary freezing of the system. A different stopping point could and generally does produce a quite different picture of the phenomenon: a still-life picture or representation of a process is simply inadequate. Take the case in which still-life pictures were used to describe a troubled marriage. The marriage, characterized by the husband's passive withdrawal and the wife's nagging criticism, was viewed in quite different ways by the partners. The wife saw her nagging as a reaction to her husband's withdrawal. On the other hand, the husband viewed his withdrawal as a defense against his wife's nagging. Who caused what? Each partner was stopping the on-going communication process to make a cause-effect conclusion that favored his/her innocence. In so doing, each distorted the actual process of communication.

The process viewpoint just presented contends that each participant in social interaction communicates with and affects the other and is affected by numerous continually changing forces. But it is clear that both participants are continually participating in this interaction. It is not accurate, therefore, to view such interaction as an on-off, let's-take-turns exchange. Rather, "all persons are engaged in sending (encoding) and receiving (decoding) messages *simultaneously*. Each person is constantly *sharing* in the encoding and decoding process, and each person is *affecting* the other" (Wenburg and Wilmot, 1973, p. 5). Communication and social influence are both characterized by *continually active interaction*. What you do, (yawn, laugh, show interest, etc.) for example, while the other person is talking affects the interaction as much as when you are speaking.

Both Are Inevitable. Few individuals avoid the minimum social situation. Indeed, man continually seeks at least this minimal condition of human interaction in which one individual is within the perceptual field of another. Once this minimal social situation obtains, two processes are inevitable—communication and social influence (Watzlawick, Beavin, and Jackson, 1967).

Behavior has no opposite. One cannot think of an antonym to behavior, with the possible exception of death. Thus, if one is alive, "one cannot not behave." Furthermore, all behavior has potential message value. That is, behavior has the potential of having others attach significance or meaning to it. Thus, if all behavior *can* communicate and man cannot avoid behaving, "one cannot not communicate." What, for example, could you do in response to your fiancé's question "Do you love me?" that would not have meaning attached to it? Obviously, anything you said would have importance. What if you ignored the question? What if you laughed? Cried? Ran away? Hit her? Indeed, one cannot not communicate, as much as you might want to on occasion.

Not all behavior *does* communicate, but man must operate as if it did. Simply, the sender cannot control the behavior to which a receiver will attach meaning. An accidental burp in public, for example, may not have been heard or might have been heard and ignored, but most of us blush a little because it is possible that it might have communicated something about us. Unfortunately, we can't control whether it does, in fact, communicate or not. Therefore, since all behavior has the potential of communicating, and the determination of those behaviors which do communicate rests solely with the receiver, the sender must accept the possibility that all of his behavior is communicating. For example, the fact that you may have an unusual "tic" or eye twitch is probably of little import to most, but a psychiatrist will probably attach great significance to such a quirk. This fact of social interaction puts man in a position similar to that of the advertising executive who once remarked that he knew that 50 percent of his advertising was ineffective, but since he didn't know which 50 percent it was, he was forced to continue running all of it. In sum, man simply cannot "turn off" communication as he can a water faucet.

If communication is usually inevitable, so is influence. "To say that influence occurs is to insist that some necessary effects, outcomes, or consequences function as defining attributes of communication" (Mortensen, 1972, p. 357). Even if communication does not result in gross behavioral change or drastic opinion modification, the perception of behavior and assignment of meaning to that behavior "has an accumulative impact on the meaning of *whatever* is said and done" (Mortensen, 1972, p. 358). Meaning is learned through experiences with the symbol, and each experience with symbolic behavior refines the meaning of that symbol. Thus, whether subtle or drastic, communication cannot avoid changing the state of the receiving organism: one cannot not influence. What, for example, would you think if you walked into a lecture hall and all of the students were sound asleep? Wouldn't you conclude that the lecture was boring and then either leave or join the crowd and take a nap? What if all the students were on the edge of their seats in concentrated attention? Wouldn't you probably stay and see what was so interesting? Is there any behavior of that audience that wouldn't have meaning for you and at least partially determine (influence) your behavior?

When man enters a minimal social situation and attempts to understand the situation by attaching meaning or some interpretation to the objects of his social environment, communication and social influence are inevitable.

Both Are Receiver Phenomena. For communication and social influence to occur, the *receiver* must be affected. *The receiver* assigns meaning to behavior. *The receiver* changes. Alternatively, one could assert that neither communication nor social influence is a sender phenomenon; try as one will, neither communication nor social influence will occur without another individual.* These concepts differ, it should be noted, from concepts such as "love," "hate," or "envy." One can love, hate, or envy another without the object of one's emotion being aware of the emotion. Furthermore, the fact that the object of one's emotion is unaware of its existence in no way diminishes the reality of the feeling. Social influence and communication, on the other hand, take place *in* the receiver.

If you saw one of your professors downtown, for instance, and said "Hi" to him and he failed to respond, you might well conclude that he ignored you on purpose. Your anger at this rebuff might result in your skipping that professor's class for a week. Now both the meaning assigned to the behavior and the ultimate influence of the social slight were due to and took place within you. The communication ("He hates me") and the influence (skipping class) occurred in the receiver. This example illustrates two additional characteristics of social influence and communication which will determine the way each process is viewed. First, the intention of the communicator, or influencer, is irrelevant to the determination of the existence of the process.† Communication has occurred, whether or not one intends to communicate with another, if the receiver attaches

---

*Of course, we do communicate with ourselves—*intrapersonal* communication. In this case, however, an individual is functioning as both source and receiver.

†The intention of the sender does become relevant, however, in the determination of success, the correspondence between the desired and the achieved outcomes.

meaning to the communicator's behavior. Though probably unintentionally, your professor communicated with and influenced you. Second, in neither communication nor social influence is the receiver a passive respondent; rather, he is actively involved. The receiver does not merely react to the behavior in his perceptual field as an amoeba does to light; he activates his entire person in the process of interpretation. In so doing, the meaning ultimately attached to a perception and any resultant change in internal state are as much a result of the individual himself as is the environment which initiated the need for interpretation. That is, one's psychological environment is, functionally, only that which he created. To digress for a moment, if you were predisposed to like that particular professor in the first place, you might have interpreted the professor's behavior as reflecting the fact that he didn't hear you say "hi." If that meaning was assigned to the behavior, you probably would not have been influenced to skip class. Behavior does not carry inherent communicative meaning or necessary influence; both are the products of an active perceiver.

Both Are Context-Bound. Neither communication nor social influence can exist independent of context. Just as one cannot give a speech without content (despite the apparent attempts by some politicians to do just that), social influence must occur someplace. Researchers and theorists in both communication and social influence have recognized this characteristic of social interaction. Referring to the process of persuasion, Fotheringham (1966) remarked, "Contextual factors, rather than the message, often become the major determinants of response" (p. 46). Brockreide (1970) noted that the rhetorical act is the interrelationship of "interpersonal, attitudinal, and situational factors" (p. 26). Eskola (1961), in a study of social influence, asserted that "the fact that x exerts influence on y in a situation z can be expressed through the three-termed sentential function xyz (x influences y in situation z). Influence itself (V_{xyz}) is consequently a function of three factors" (p. 22).

What happens when the context is changed? Isn't it probable that a sergeant would get a different reaction from a private to the command "Do 30 push-ups!" when they were both on duty than when they were both in a tavern in town? Is telling "a little white lie" the same at a cocktail party as it is in a courtroom? Would you prefer to solicit funds for cancer research by going door to door in your neighborhood or by making your "pitch" to visitors to a cancer research and treatment facility? Obviously, context affects the processes of social influence and communication.

There are at least two readily identifiable contexts—the physical context (those objectively verifiable factors such as room color, furniture arrangement, temperature, etc.) and the functional context (the perception and interpretation of the physical context plus the psychological, sociological, and cultural environment that each individual brought to the immediate situation). As will be demonstrated throughout this book, not only is it possible for both types of contexts to alter the processes of communication and social influence, but often the context can almost totally account for observed behavior. Understanding when the context, either physical or functional, inhibits, complements, or obviates the processes of communication and social influence is one of the major goals of this book.

Communication and Social Influence: Isomorphic Processes

To this point we have arrived at the following conclusions:

1. Social influence cannot occur without communication.

2. Social influence is the inevitable result of communication.

3. Communication is the process of assigning meaning to behavior.

4. Social influence is the process by which the behavior of one or more individuals induces change in the state of another individual or group of individuals.

5. Both social influence and communication:
   a) are transactional processes.
   b) are inevitable in social situations.
   c) are receiver phenomena.
   d) are context-bound processes.

Are these processes really one process masquerading as two separate, independent processes? Are they functionally equivalent? Has academia been duplicating efforts by studying the car on one hand and the automobile on the other? Or, is one process a subset of the other, as a terrier is a subset of the class of dogs? Does one process focus on means and the other on ends? Obviously, the answers to these questions are crucial to further investigation.

The concept of social influence includes all instances in which the behavior of one person induces changes in the state of another person. To do so, however, the behavior of the first individual must be attended to and have meaning attached to it by another, which is the minimal condition of communication. Therefore, all social influence involves communication. For example, earlier in this chapter Clyde was influenced by four confederates of an experimenter, but only because those four behaved in a way that meant something to Clyde—they said "C." Could the other four have influenced Clyde without doing something Clyde wouldn't interpret or attach meaning to? Probably not.

Similarly, as communication inevitably results in the alteration of the state of the individual perceiver, all communication involves social influence. Even if it is only the addition to a person's experience with a symbol, all communication influences. Thus, just as a consideration of dominance involves the consideration of submissiveness, and vice versa, *the processes of communication and social influence are isomorphic, or equivalent.* They are inseparable aspects of an undifferentiated social process and will, therefore, be considered as one for the remainder of this book.

THE SOURCES OF SOCIAL INFLUENCE: A MODEL

If we want to understand the process of social influence, we must explore all the sources of influences operating on an individual during social interaction. For example, to conclude that Clyde was influenced by the four confederates during the conformity experiment would be accurate but incomplete. Clearly, the level of confidence Clyde felt as a function of the task affected his yielding. Furthermore, the relationship between Clyde and the other group members altered the amount of influence. Had they been six years old, for instance, Clyde would probably not have been influenced. Suffice it to say, many factors contributed to Clyde's being influenced. Thus, a model of influence is needed to assist in the identification of the sources of influence.

A model of social influence, however, must be based on a few initial assumptions:

1. It must accommodate the nature of process. The dynamic interaction of a wide variety of factors involved in social influence must not be so distorted that the process appears linear or mechanistic.

2. It must be based on a psychological approach. Behavior must be described in subjective, experiential, personal, or phenomenal, as well as objective, terms. Influences on an individual should not be described just in objective physicalistic terms, but also "in the way in which it exists for that person at that time" (Lewin, 1951, p. 62). "That is, the situation must be described from the viewpoint of the individual whose behavior is under consideration, rather than from the viewpoint of the observer" (Shaw and Costanzo, 1970, p. 119). Barnlund stated the point another way: "It is not events themselves, but how men construe events, that determines what they will see, what they will think, and how they will respond" (1968, p. 25).

3. It must reflect accurately the tremendous breadth of sources of potential influence. That is, it must not be limited by such narrow points of view as those that created the false impression of the importance of messages or media. To accomplish this breadth of perspective, the model must start not with "picking out one or another isolated elements within the situation as a whole," but with a characterization of the situation as a whole. "After this first approximation, the various aspects and parts of the situation undergo a more and more specific and detailed analysis. It is obvious that such a method is the best safeguard against being mislead by one or another element of the situation" (Lewin, 1951, p. 63).

In keeping with these requirements, the following model (Fig. 1–1) of the sources of social influence is offered.

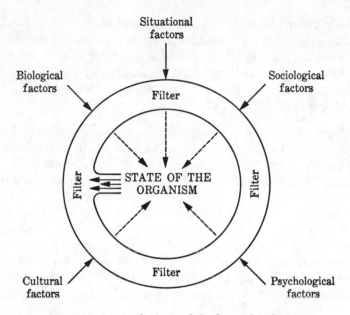

Fig. 1–1 An analytic model of social influence.

Influence Factors

The following examples illustrate the nature of these classes of social influence.

1. Sociological factors (self/other) include all relationships between people: power, trust, leadership, status, anonymity, attraction, similarity, credibility, role, membership group, reference group, etc.
2. Psychological factors (self) include such factors as attitude, ego-involvement, dogmatism, beliefs, values, personality, self-esteem, motivation, linguistic facility, intelligence, etc.
3. Cultural factors (self/society) include such factors as language, religion, norms, laws, philosophy, values, government, prejudices, food habits, etc.
4. Biological factors (self/heredity) include such factors as intelligence, sex, race, age, size, birth order, perceptual ability, psychomotor coordination, physical features, etc.

5. Situational factors (self/situation) include all factors related to a specific time-space loci or situation, the unfolding events of a spatial and temporal present, such as time, location, physical setting, temperature, purpose, participants, behavior, message, atmosphere, speaker, topic, media, financial status, etc.

These five general classes of potentially influencing forces are neither exhaustive nor mutually exclusive. In fact, it is virtually self-evident that each group of factors interacts with the others and that the effect of any given factor may be a function of one or more of the others. For example, factors of your culture may well interact with your relationship with others; or, your biological make-up might affect the way in which you interact with the environment. Additionally, not all factors can be assumed to be equally important in every circumstance. Nevertheless, it will prove useful to use the broad classification of influencing factors to analyze instances of social influence.

Filter

The model shows the external influencing forces passing through a "filter." "Filter," of course, is not the best word to describe an active process, as it implies a passive screening function, but it will serve. The existence of this filter is a manifestation of man actively affecting or participating in his environment. The nature and operation of this filter vary from individual to individual. A person's perception, culture, abilities, attitudes, values, prejudices, experience, self-concept—the entire person—determine the character of this filter. The model demonstrates this total involvement of the person by indicating the origin of the filter at the "state of the organism." The effects of this filter are numerous—selective exposure, distorted perception, selective attention, attribution of causality and responsibility, to name but a few. The importance of this filter was noted by Hastorf, Schneider, and Polefka (1970): "*The research in person perception has shifted in interest from the stimuli and the accuracy with which they are recorded to the ways that perceivers actively process those stimuli to create interpersonal meaning*" (p. 91).

An example of this filter in operation may help to explain its nature. If a group of prejudiced white students and a group of nonprejudiced white students are shown a picture of a white man holding a knife on a black man by means of a tachistoscope, (a device that flashes a picture *very* quickly on a screen), they will give different reports of what they saw. The prejudiced subjects will often report that they saw a black man holding a knife on a white man. But when physiological measures are examined to see if they are telling the truth about what they thought they saw, it is discovered that they are accurately reporting what they thought they saw. In short, their filter so distorted the image that they *actually believed* they saw the reverse of what was physically present in the picture. Nonprejudiced students, on the other hand, typically report accurately what the picture presented; their psychological state did not necessitate restructuring reality. The product of this filter is the phenomenal, or psychological, reality that operates on individual behavior.

Psychological Reality

The dotted lines toward the center of the model represent the "reality" created by the individual. This is the world as it exists for an individual. These forces, and these forces alone, comprise the contemporaneous reality for any individual that induces change in the state of the organism. This constructed reality is as much a function of the organism doing the creating as is the environmental or external stimulation. The correspondence between the external stimuli and the received reality is frequently poor, as the example of the prejudiced subjects just reviewed indicates. To cite another example of this lack of correspondence between internal and external reality, one need only refer to a common, everyday experience. When you sit in a lecture hall with a noisy air conditioning system (if you are lucky enough to have *any* air conditioning), you frequently become habituated to the "hum," and the "hum," though an objectively present stimulus, becomes irrelevant—a psychological nonentity. It is the personal or psychological reality that impinges on human behavior and induces change. How often have you been pleased or angered by what you thought someone said, only to find out that you misunderstood? Until you found out that you misunderstood, the constructed reality was "real," and the "real" message, what was said, was irrelevant.

EFFECTS OF SOCIAL INFLUENCE

The model just presented showed "the state of the organism" as the target of the factors of influence. Obviously, the "state of the organism" can be influenced in a variety of ways. One could usefully assert that there are short-term and long-term effects, observable and unobservable effects, relevant and irrelevant effects, major and minor effects. Each of these distinctions casts light on the nature of the impact of social influence. However, to try to simultaneously maintain or consider all potential classifications of effects would be impossible. Therefore, three descriptive classes of effects or changes in "the state of the organism" will be advanced:

1. Cognitive changes—alteration of knowledge, belief, or conception about some aspect of the environment.

2. Psychological changes—alteration of attitudes, motivations, values, or feelings toward some aspect of the environment.

3. Behavioral changes—alteration of overt behavior toward some aspect of the environment.

It must be remembered that all of these changes are *process changes*. That is, they are not analogous to physical changes such as the transformation of water into ice or the alteration of a bumper in an auto accident, both of which involve a set of temporally discrete events. Rather, process changes result from the interaction of a large number of variables without easily defined beginnings or endings. Indeed, because process change has an almost kinetic quality, one might refer to it as *changing* rather than change.

TYPES OF SOCIAL INFLUENCE

The preceding model suggests that social influence is a complex phenomenon, with many factors involved in its operation. Probably one of the best ways to understand this complicated process is to examine specific types of social influence. There have been a variety of attempts to theoretically distinguish among types of social influence and still preserve its fundamental complexity. Some attempts, such as Kelman's (1961) and Coleman's (1963), have greatly aided in dealing conceptually with the tremendous scope of social influence behaviors. Others, such as those that focus on the topic or message differences, have caused a myopic view that fosters the belief that the message is the dominant factor in social influence.

One of the most insightful attempts to differentiate the multidimensional process of social influence was offered by Deutsch and Gerard (1955).* They identified two types of social influence—informational social influence and normative social influence. "An *informational social influence* may be defined as an influence to accept information obtained from another as *evidence* about reality" (p. 629). When one individual accepts another's behavior as a valid source of information about reality, informational social influence has occurred. Informational social influence (ISI) is largely self-inflicted; it occurs when another's behavior is attended to and has impact as the result of the perceiver's trying to be "correct" or "appropriate." Most ISI is from a source who is not intentionally seeking to influence. For example, if one student observes another student who is known to be "bright" mark "C" to a test question and the first student follows suit (cheats), informational social influence has occurred. The bright student did not attempt to affect his classmate, but his behavior was used as "evidence about reality." In this sense, ISI is *consummatory*, as "the need for order and stability, the search for relevant information as a means of reducing uncertainty, tends to be pursued as an end in itself" (Mortensen, 1972, p. 369).

Normative social influence, on the other hand, is "an influence to conform with the positive expectations of another" (Deutsch and Gerard, 1955, p. 629). Normative social influence (NSI) results because of a desire by the receiver to achieve

---

*The distinction offered by Deutsch and Gerard relies heavily on Festinger (1950) and Kelly (1952) and is similar to the theoretical distinctions proposed by Thibaut and Strickland (1956). The theoretical distinctions in this book are very similar, but not identical to the treatment of this issue by Deutsch and Gerard.

something beyond merely being correct. In short, NSI is largely *instrumental*, as the thought or action influenced is affected because change is seen as a means to a desired goal—being liked, getting a promotion, making money, etc. Most NSI is from a source who is intentionally seeking to influence. For example, if a parent tries to influence a child to study by threatening the child with punishment, the influenced behavior, studying, would probably be viewed by the child as instrumental—by studying he would avoid punishment.

ISI and NSI types of social influence exist on a continuum in reality. Seldom does a pure form of either type of influence occur; most situations involve some of both types of influence. For example, earlier in this chapter Clyde used the behavior of the other four students to assist him in defining, or arriving at, the correct answer on the line-matching problem, but he also may have wanted to be liked by the others and thus viewed conformity as a means of achieving that goal. The former motivation, the desire to be correct, is generally involved in ISI, whereas the latter motivation, a desire to be liked, is generally involved in NSI. Clyde's act of conformity illustrates that any given instance of social influence is probably the result of both normative and informational influences processes. Nevertheless, it will prove useful for our analysis to consider the processes independently.

To summarize the types of social influence discussed so far:

1. Informational social influence (ISI) is influence which occurs when the recipient *uses* the behavior of others to assist him in arriving at a decision. Generally, ISI is unintended by the source.

2. Normative social influence (NSI) is influence which occurs when the receiver accepts influence *in order to* gain some desired goal. Generally, NSI is intended by the source.

Within this classification of normative social influence, there appear to be two functionally separate sets of conditions. Specifically, normative social influence includes both situations in which another person exerts expectations on an individual *and* those situations in which an individual exerts expectations on himself. Let's expand on the first situation.

When one individual exerts expectations on another, there is generally an outcome that the influencer controls. For example, when an employer tells his employee to shave off his beard, a union representative demands concessions of management, or a professor assigns a paper, if these expectations are met the result may be a promotion, satisfactory labor-management relations, or a good grade. If they are not met, the result might be a firing, a strike, or a failing grade. In each of these instances one person has power to control the rewards or punishments of the other for compliance or noncompliance—he has *outcome control* over another. This type of influence involves an exchange of thought or action for reward or punishment. This is *normative social influence based on outcome control.*

Frequently, on the other hand, individuals reward *themselves* in normative social situations. For instance, all of us, as a product of our socialization, have internalized norms of thought or action. That is, we all have habits, routines, and expectations of self that occur dependably whenever the appropriate cues set them off, such as men standing when a woman enters the room. If another individual knew these dispositions, he could provide the stimuli that would elicit the pre-established pattern of thought or action. For example, advertisers obviously want you to buy their products, but they have very little opportunity to directly reward you for purchasing their product. If they knew enough about you, however, to know that you associate the color yellow with "freshness" and "wholesomeness," for example, and therefore packaged their Instant Lump cereal in a yellow box, they would be providing a *cue* to set off a predetermined response in you. Similarly, most of us are disposed to appear internally consistent in our beliefs, and one persuasive technique may well be the provision of cues that make salient the desire for consistency which would result in attitude change. This is *normative influence based on cue control.* Rather than the exchange of rewards and behavior involved in outcome control, cue control relies on the *arousal* of pre-existing patterns of thought and action and self-administered rewards.

The distinctions between normative social influence based on outcome control and that based on cue control will be made more evident in the next three chapters. At this point, however, you should note that both types of NSI are, generally, intentionally designed on the part of one individual to induce change in another.

ORGANIZATION OF THE BOOK

The chapters of this book are designed to reflect the organization dictated by the types of social influence just identified. The next three chapters describe and analyze social influence from three functionally distinct perspectives. Chapter Two, "Informational Social Influence," focuses on the nature of informational social influence and the factors which inhibit, contribute, or modify the impact of the primary message. Chapter Three, "Normative Social Influence: Outcome Control," similarly treats that process of influence. Normative social influence based on cue control is analyzed in Chapter Four. At the conclusion of Chapters Two, Three, and Four a set of summary propositions is presented, indicating the current state of knowledge about the type of influence discussed. Chapter Five shifts the focus from description to prescription. In this chapter we will explore the various practices recommended "when you become the manipulator."

SUMMARY

The task and the method of our study are now set. The pervasive process of social influence has been characterized as a transactional process, as an inevitable result of man's social environment, as a receiver phenomenon, and as a process dependent on its context for meaning. Additionally, social influence was shown to be isomorphic with the process of communication. Five sources of influence were identified: biological, psychological, sociological, cultural, and situational. Social influence was found to result in three general classes of dynamic impact: cognitive, psychological, and behavioral. Finally, the process of social influence was differentiated into three subprocesses: informational social influence, normative social influence: outcome control, and normative social influence: cue control.

Chapter Two

Informational
Social Influence

Every evening millions of Americans rely on network television news as their sole window on national and world affairs. Most viewers accept the evening reports as providing factual evidence about the reality of the past day's events; that is, they assume the "objectivity" of the newscasters. Clearly, however, the same event can be reported in many ways, as the headlines of the following two fictitious newscasts illustrate:

NOV. 1

> Newscast #1: Police riot in Florida—24 students injured
>
> Newscast #2: Three police injured in breakup of beach drug party

NOV. 2

> Newscast #1: CIA attempt to assassinate Latin American leader uncovered
>
> Newscast #2: Communist coup thwarted in Latin America

NOV. 3

> Newscast #1: Supreme Court affirms defendant's right to counsel
>
> Newscast #2: Convicted murderer gets off on technicality

NOV. 4

> Newscast #1: Parole found more effective than prison in reducing repetition rate
>
> Newscast #2: 60% of parolees return to prison

NOV. 5

> Newscast #1: Increase in crime rate slowed last year
>
> Newscast #2: Major crimes up 14% last year

There is little doubt that the attitudes of those viewers who relied on a steady diet of newscast #1 would differ from those who consistently listened to newscast #2. For example, which viewing audience would probably be more predisposed to vote for increased police power?

In the preceding example, neither newscaster perceived himself, nor was he perceived by his viewers, as attempting to influence. Rather, the two newscasters and their listeners assumed that the newscasts functioned purely to disseminate information. Nevertheless, influence probably occurred—*informational social influence.*

THE NATURE OF INFORMATIONAL SOCIAL INFLUENCE

Informational social influence (ISI) is nonmanipulative. This form of influence is entirely dependent on the receiver. It occurs when one individual uses the behavior of another to assist him in determining his own thought or action. Generally, the source of the influence does not intentionally attempt to influence or manipulate the person influenced; indeed, he may not even know that his behavior is being observed. For example, when faced with five forks at a formal dinner, you may have little idea of the correct etiquette, but you would not want to make a fool of yourself. Therefore, you would probably observe the behavior of the most urbane diner and follow his lead. Note that the sophisticated guest did not direct an influence attempt toward you, but his behavior, whether correct or not, was imitated. He provided information, and thereby, he influenced. This example illustrates the two bases of informational social influence (ISI): *information dependence* and *motivation to save face.*

Information Dependence

Information dependence begins at birth. A child is brought into a world with which he is hopelessly incapable of dealing by himself. His parents dictate and structure his behavior as a baby. But as the child grows and becomes capable of independent behavior, his need for information about his environment grows. However, the amount of information needed for independent behavior grows faster than the child's ability to acquire that information firsthand. Therefore, a child becomes increasingly reliant on others (e.g., teachers, parents, books, television, etc.) for information about his world. Jones and Gerard (1967) noted that "one fact that highlights man's uniqueness in the animal kingdom is the high proportion of information that is mediated by others" (p. 127). In fact, were it not for man's ability to use information provided by others about the world, his behavior would be largely trial and error; his knowledge limited to direct experience. In sum, the socialization process is, in part, a period of teaching children how to rely on others for information about the world—to become information dependent.

The now-classic study by Schacter and Singer (1962) demonstrates well the role of information dependence in social influence. These researchers investigated the extent to which we rely on others in the labeling of our own emotions. They artificially induced in the subjects a physiological state common to many emotions (heightened heart and respiration rate and so on) and then allowed them to wait for further instructions with another person who had presumably received the same treatment. The persons with whom the subjects waited were, in fact, confederates of the researchers. Some of the subjects waited with confederates who exhibited behavior associated with the emotion of anger; others waited with confederates who behaved as if they were joyous. The subjects, who felt a physiological state of emotion but lacked a corresponding psychological interpretation, reported that they felt happy when in the room with the happy confederate or angry if they waited with the angry confederate. Clearly, the subjects in this experiment needed information ("This isn't a normal feeling, what is it?") and used the behavior of others in determining the interpretation of their own feelings.

Face-Saving

Whether trying to choose the correct fork at a formal party or the appropriate emotional response to a situation, each individual is motivated to "save face" in social situations. Goffman noted (1968) that an individual, "by repeatedly and automatically asking himself the question 'If I do or do not act in this way, will I or others lose face?'" decides "at each moment, consciously or unconsciously, how to behave" (p. 322). That man is motivated by a desire to save face in social situations is evident; the characteristics and types of "face-saving" behaviors, however, are not fully understood. Brown and Garland (1971) investigated the effects of face-saving in a very typical situation. They had subjects sing and then told some of them that they were good singers and others that they were bad singers. The subjects then had to sing in public in front of either strangers or peers. Naturally, those told that they were poor singers behaved in ways to minimize loss of face (i.e., they sang only a short while), especially when the observers were peers. Despite the situational complexity of this motive, the following appear to be some of the submotives of the face-saving complex:

1. desire to appear competent
2. desire to be right
3. desire to avoid embarrassment
4. desire to protect self-esteem
5. desire to be liked.

A whole series of studies in an area of research generally called "social facilitation" demonstrates the pervasiveness of man's motivation to save face. Social-facilitation research is based on two experimental models—audience effects and coaction effects. The first model examines behavior when it occurs in the presence of passive observers. The second research area examines behavior when it occurs in the presence of another individual or group of individuals engaged in the same activity. Research in audience effects has found that the presence of a passive observer generally increases or improves the performance of simple or well-learned tasks, such as multiplication (Dashiell, 1930). That is, people do more accurate multiplications when observed than when doing them alone. It appears that the presence of another individual elicits the desire to appear competent, a face-saving motive, and therefore facilitates the accomplishment of such tasks. On other tasks, however, such as learning nonsense syllables or learning a maze, the presence of spectators decreased performance (Pessin and Husband, 1933).

These apparently contradictory data remained a paradox until 1965, when Zajonc advanced a relatively simple explanation. He argued that "the emission of well-learned responses is facilitated by the presence of spectators, while the acquisition of new responses is impaired" (p. 270). That is, performance is enhanced, whereas learning is impaired by the presence of passive observers. Zajonc further simplified this explanation by concluding that since the dominant (most probable) response for a well-learned task is generally correct, whereas the dominant response during learning is generally incorrect, the "audience enhances the emission of dominant responses" (p. 270). This explanation has been put to experimental tests and found to be accurate (Zajonc and Sales, 1966).

All of this would have little relevance to a discussion of face-saving were it not that the reason individuals emit dominant responses when observed is that they desire to appear competent or, conversely, they are apprehensive of evaluation. That is, when individuals are observed, they want to appear competent; therefore, they do what they think will result in saving face. Fortunately, when the task is a simple one, this motive probably will result in saving face, because the dominant response is usually correct. But when the task is difficult or unlearned, the dominant response is usually incorrect, and the motivation to save face will probably result in decreased performance. In short, the audience effect occurs because people desire to save face (Cottrell, 1968; Henchy and Glass, 1968).

The research in coaction, the second experimental model in the social-facilitation research area, demonstrates similar conclusions. For example, when individuals accomplish such simple tasks as multiplication and vowel cancellations in long lists of words, they perform better with others doing the same task than when working alone. However, when working on an intellectual, problem-solving task, individuals performed better alone than in groups. Thus, Zajonc concluded, "the generalization which organizes these results is that the presence of others, as spectators or as coactors, enhances the emission of dominant responses" (p. 273).

Man is motivated to save face. This strong motive contributes to the working of informational social influence, as "it is this striving to be right that motivates people to pay close attention to what other people are doing" (Aronson, 1972, p. 94). The observation of another's behavior serves as a benchmark, or guide, for one's own thought or action. Kiesler and Kiesler (1969) summarized the relationship of face-saving and ISI in this way: "People apparently develop a strong need to be personally and socially 'correct' in their behavior and opinions. ... one easy definition of correctness is the behavior of relevant others" (p. 44).

The Crucial Variable: Uncertainty

Because of man's learned information dependence and desire to save face, ISI is a pervasive type of social influence. The circumstances under which man's information dependence and his desire to save face are greatest are those in which he is uncertain. When an individual is uncertain, he (1) risks the possibility of losing face and is, therefore, motivated to save face, and (2) becomes more dependent on others for information. Thus, the crucial variable in ISI is the level of uncertainty experienced by an individual in any given social situation; the greater the uncertainty, the greater the probability of ISI, because "the natural response to ambiguity is to seek clarifying information" (Jones and Gerard, 1967, p. 15). It could be argued, therefore, that teachers foster cheating by asking difficult questions. Tough questions make a student uncertain and highly susceptible to information provided by other students' tests.

Thus, our task is clear. To understand the nature and operation of ISI we must answer the following types of questions:

1. What factors increase uncertainty?
2. What and whose behavior will be utilized to reduce uncertainty?
3. Are there individual differences in degree of information dependence? When? Why?
4. Are there individual differences in the strength of the motivation to save face? When? Why?

ISI REVISITED

To find answers to these and other questions about the nature and operation of ISI, a variety of research areas must be examined. The ISI phenomenon has been divided into a great number of relatively isolated research concerns, among them:

imitation, observational learning, bystander intervention, identification, contagion, modeling, internalization, and conformity. It is beyond the scope of this book to review the theoretical and definitional bases for the differentiation of these processes, the findings associated with each area of research, and the theories proposed to account for the finding associated with each area of research. Additionally, it may be questioned whether separate examination of each research area benefits scientific inquiry into ISI. If imitation, conformity, modeling, and so on are all governed by the same determinants and have similar consequences, independent research of each area may cause needless confusion. It may even retard the advance of knowledge because of unnecessary duplication of efforts. Indeed, research does indicate that the determinants of the variety of ISI subprocesses are very similar. Therefore, rather than examine each separate area of ISI research, this chapter will consider as ISI all those social situations in which:

1. an individual observes and attaches meaning to the behavior of another individual or group of individuals

2. the behavior observed is relevant to a felt uncertainty in the observer

3. the behavior observed is used by the observer to assist him in determining his own attitude, belief, or behavior.

When a social situation meets these criteria, it is an example of ISI, whether some would call it "conformity," "imitation," or some other more restrictive name.

Before proceeding, an important question must be considered: What constitutes the message in ISI? The message, put simply, is the need-relevant behavior of the influencer. In other words, the message is the behavior that is related to the felt uncertainty of the observer. Or, as Mortensen (1972) suggests, the message *"consists of whatever unit of behavior serves to link the parties of communication"* (p. 19). For example, when you were choosing among five forks, you needed information, and the behavior of another person had meaning for you. That behavior, the other's choice of a specific fork, "said," "I know what I'm doing; I've been to hundreds of formal dinners, and one always begins with the outside fork." His behavior is as clear, unequivocal, and reliably interpreted as the display of the peace sign or a clenched fist. In sum, the message in ISI is the need-relevant behavior of the influencer.

The remainder of this chapter will be organized according to the model presented in Chapter One. Specifically, we will look at the psychological, sociological, situational, cultural, and biological variables that affect the probability of ISI occurring.

PSYCHOLOGICAL FACTORS

When you are in the presence of another person and influence him without intending to, the degree of influence depends more on him than on you. As already indicated, the psychological make-up of the person influenced is critical of the influence process. Research has investigated the effects of such psychological factors as self-esteem, intelligence, self-confidence, authoritarianism, acquiescence, anxiety, commitment, ego-involvement, need for affiliation, need for social approval, and need for achievement. An example may illustrate how these psychological factors affect ISI.

If a highly intelligent person and one not so blessed were faced with a group that disagreed with their decision about some judgment task (e.g., which painting is more beautiful, or which person would be the best employee), the less intelligent person would probably be influenced by the opposing majority's decision, whereas the more intelligent individual would probably not (Crutchfield, 1955; Wyer, 1967). The intelligent person was not affected, in part, because he perceived himself as capable of making the judgment decision independent of, or in spite of, the discrepant information provided by others and was, therefore, not dependent on others for information about reality. On the other hand, the less intelligent person was faced with an opposing majority, felt uncertain, and was dependent on others for information; the increased information dependence resulted in the less intelligent person's being susceptible to ISI. Thus, the degree of dependence alters the amount of influence.

An individual's information dependence on others is, in part, a function of how he feels about his abilities. It is, therefore, not surprising to find that individuals of typically low self-esteem are more susceptible to ISI than are persons of high self-esteem (League and Jackson, 1964). Not only does the general personality trait of self-esteem affect ISI, but so does task-specific self-esteem. Numerous studies (Ettinger, *et al.*, 1971; Goldberg and Lubin, 1958; Mausner, 1954; Samelson, 1957) have induced subjects to believe that they had an unusual ability to make certain types of judgments; these subjects were less influenced by the knowledge of an opposing judgment by others than were subjects who had not been told that they were unusually talented. In one such study (Snyder, Mischel, and Lott, 1960) the researchers gave some subjects information designed to make them "experts" on a given topic; those subjects were less influenced than those not given the expert-producing information when faced with discrepant information.

Another way in which subjects have been led to be confident in their own ability is to allow them prior success on some judgment task. Situations designed to make a subject succeed on a judgment task apparently increased their confidence and reduced their information dependence, which resulted in a reduction in their susceptibility to ISI. Repeated task-specific success reduced an individual's susceptibility to ISI.

Your own observations probably support this finding. Is the student with a good grade-point average or the student with a low g.p.a. more likely to cheat? The successful student is probably more confident in his own ability and is, therefore, less likely to rely on the judgments of others. (Or possibly, he is more confident in his ability to cheat, thus making him more likely to cheat but less likely to get caught.) In sum, if an individual has high self-esteem or some reason to be confident in his own ability or opinion (e.g., perceives himself to be intelligent, or an expert, or has experienced prior success), he will be more likely to rely on himself and correspondingly less likely to be influenced by information provided by the behavior of others.

Perceived relative competence of self and others also determines, in part, who a person will use as an information source. Put simply, people are informationally influenced by people perceived as relatively more "able" than themselves

(Britt, 1971). Again, let's use the cheating example. If while taking a test, a person was sitting between a person he thought was intelligent and one he thought was dull, whose behavior would have greater value to him?

Another personality variable that affects susceptibility to ISI is authoritarianism. A person characterized as a high-authoritarian is one who consistently refers to "authorities" in the evaluation and determination of his own decisions, opinions, and behavior. The high-authoritarian person is information dependent on authorities and is, therefore, more susceptible to ISI than is his low-authoritarian counterpart (Beloff, 1958; Crutchfield, 1955; Nadler, 1959). Not only are high-authoritarians more easily influenced by authorities than are low-authoritarians, some individuals, as Frye and Bass (1963) assert, are simply predisposed to acquiesce or be submissive. Persons who possess this personality trait are obviously more susceptible to ISI (Bass, 1956).

Anxiety, the psychological and physiological correlate of uncertainty, is also related to susceptibility to ISI. Quite simply, in the continual attempt to resolve anxiety, the anxious person is more receptive to information that may alleviate his anxiety. This rather uncritical acceptance of information results in the anxious person's being more frequently influenced than the nonanxious person (Kogan and Wallach, 1967; Meunier and Rule, 1967). Isn't the uncertain student anxious when taking a test? It looks more and more as if teachers maximize the probability of cheating.

Two variables, commitment and ego-involvement, have been demonstrated to affect ISI by affecting the confidence an individual feels in the correctness of his attitudes or beliefs or in his ability. Specifically, when an individual is committed to a belief, attitude, or action or is ego-involved with his position on some issue, he becomes more confident in his belief, attitude, or action and less dependent on others for information. As with the variables discussed previously, reduced information dependence decreases susceptibility to ISI. For example, place yourself in the following situation. You and your friend both decide that you favor candidate X. However, you decide to work for candidate X, whereas your friend merely waits for election day so he can vote for candidate X. After two weeks of doorbelling for your candidate, you and your friend hear an individual you both respect indicate that he thinks that candidate X is incompetent. Is it more likely that you or your friend will be influenced by this third opinion? Research suggests that your commitment to your high regard of candidate X should make you less susceptible to influence than your friend who was not similarly committed. Did your answer correspond to that suggested by the research?

Finally, three fairly persistent types of motivations have been discovered to affect ISI. The needs for affiliation, achievement, and social approval all exist to some degree in every person. The greater the motivation, or need, for affiliation, achievement, or social approval, the greater the probability of ISI (Cottrell, 1968; Smith and Flenning, 1971). These motives are all social, and strong social motives arouse a strong desire to save face, which increases susceptibility to ISI.

To a large extent, the variables just reviewed determine the level of information dependence or motivation to save face of a given individual and thereby his susceptibility to ISI. Obviously, numerous other factors, such as those to be covered in the following pages, also affect information dependence. The next group of variables, the sociological variables affecting ISI, on the other hand, largely determine *who* an individual will be influenced by. That is, given that an individual needs information, he has many models to which he can attend and which can serve as a guide for his thought or action. The crucial question is "Whose behavior will an individual attend to and model, or imitate?"

SOCIOLOGICAL FACTORS

Many dimensions of the social relationship between the influencer and the person influenced have been explored. The nature of this relationship affects the amount of influence and determines whose behavior will be imitated. For example, it is virtually inconceivable that a middle-level executive would choose to copy or emulate the attire of an office boy rather than that of the president of the firm. We copy the behavior of those people we admire. However, as we are about to discover, the situation isn't quite that simple.

Anonymity

One of the more important sociological self-assessments is the degree of anonymity or, conversely, identifiability a person feels. When an individual feels that he and his behavior are totally anonymous, the necessity to save face, a social motive, is virtually nil ("nobody will know even if I'm wrong or appear incompetent"). On the other hand, if it is obvious that one's behavior will be very public and identified with him, the motive to save face is strong, and therefore the desire for information is maximal. Brown (1971) noted this facet of social behavior when he observed that the motive to save face is dependent on the visibility of potentially embarrassing acts. When the motive to save face is strong and the dependence on others for information is high, informational social influence is probable. Thus, as a general proposition we can conclude that the more anonymous an individual feels, the lower the probability of ISI. This conclusion has been tested in a variety of contexts.

ISI resulting in conformity is more frequent in situations in which the judgment of a subject is made public than in situations in which the subject can keep his decision to himself (Argyle, 1957; Crutchfield, 1955; Deutsch and Gerard, 1955). Consider, for example, a situation in which a number of friends at a party liked a particular movie and voiced their opinion. If one individual did not like the movie but was asked his opinion, he would more probably agree with the majority than if he was given the option of writing his opinion on a piece of paper and throwing it in the fireplace. In the latter circumstance the individual's opinion was anonymous, whereas in the former his opinion was very public.

Anonymity is also involved in an ISI phenomenon called the "risky or cautious shift." It has been a recurrent observation that groups tend to make decisions that are either more risky or more cautious than the decisions the individual members make when alone. One explanation contends that for some reason the informational cues available during group discussion are in the direction of extremity, either cautious or risky. Thus, the apparent group definition or appropriateness is in the direction of extremity, and each individual within the group is identifiable. Being highly identifiable, the individual is influenced by the extreme information, but when given the chance to voice his decision alone, anonymously, he chooses a less extreme position.

If anonymity reduces susceptibility to influence, then identifiability ought to increase it. Right? The case of Kitty Genovese, described in Chapter One, demonstrates the impact of identifiability well. Latané and Rodin (1969) investigated the apparent fact that when "there are a lot of people around, rather than increasing the likelihood that *someone* will help, actually *decreases* the likelihood that any *one* of them will help" (Aronson, p. 40). Their laboratory research led them to the conclusion that when there are many people observing an apparent emergency situation and each is aware that there are many other observers not intervening, the conclusion is reached that the appropriate response to the situation is to do nothing. Further, to violate that conclusion and aid the victim would result in very identifiable or obvious nonconformity and run the risk of serious loss of face. In short, the cues from others (note the circularity of this phenomenon) define the situation as a nonemergency and thus influence the observers to conform, in part, because to be an anticonformist would be so public and potentially damaging to face. Research supports this explanation, as anonymity is highest when an individual is alone, and in the alone condition helping behavior has been observed to be likely. On the other hand, identifiability is greatest when others are present, and unfortunately for everyone in a world of growing population, helping behavior is improbable.

An interesting contradiction to the proposition that anonymity reduces susceptibility to influence can be found in the research into contagion, a label describing the wild-firelike conformity to antisocial behavior that characterizes mobs. This research indicates that influence, conformity, is greater in large crowds than in small crowds. It would seem that a member of a large crowd is virtually anonymous and ought, therefore, to be less influenced by the behavior of others than if in a small crowd, where he is more identifiable. Some have explained contagion as the diffusion of responsibility—the more people who do something, the less responsibility any single person will bear for it. Another explanation is that people "lose themselves" in a crowd and don't perceive themselves as individuals. Regardless of the ultimate explanation, this seeming contradiction highlights the necessity of more research into all the forms of social influence to discover the underlying commonalities and to resolve contradictions.

Much of the rest of the research on the relationship between the influencer and the person influenced can be summarized, with only minor damage to theoretic subtleties, by the following proposition: People attend to and are influenced by the behavior of individuals whose traits they value positively. In other words, people are influenced by another when he is seen as having *status* or as being *attractive*. The determinants and effects of these traits are very complex, very similar, and sometimes contradictory. Nevertheless, we will explore the primary research findings about each trait to determine their effect on the ISI process.

Status

The perceived status of a stimulus or model has great impact on ISI. Generally, the greater the perceived *status differential* between the influencer and the person influenced, the greater the probability of ISI. For example, individuals imitate the behavior of high-status models more than they do neutral or low-status models (Bandura and Huston, 1961; Grusec, 1966). Groups composed of high-status persons exert greater pressure to conformity than do groups composed of neutral or low-status persons (Patel and Gordon, 1960). Finally, opinion leaders have been found to have slightly higher status than those whose opinions they influence (Berelson, Lazarsfeld, and McPhee, 1954). Clearly, in a variety of contexts, the perceived status of a model has great impact on the decision that an individual makes as to who he will use as an information source. The identification of the factors that affect the attribution of status, however, is more difficult than merely concluding that status affects influence.

Research on status occupies many shelves of most libraries, and most people agree on the symbols of status in everyday life. It appears we know about, agree on, and easily and reliably identify status. Yet, the explicit statement of the origin of status attribution is very difficult. Generally, however, status is attributed as a result of the asymmetrical, or uneven, distribution of certain personal characteristics, sentiments, behaviors, spatial relations, or symbols (Brown, 1965, p. 72). Let's examine each of these potential sources of status.

Personal Characteristics. Most people would agree that an engineer is granted greater status than a road worker; an older man, greater status than a young man; a financially successful businessman, greater status than a destitute businessman; a man from "the right side of the tracks," greater status than one from "the wrong side of the tracks." Some would even agree, despite the patent absurdity of their conclusions, that men and WASP's have greater status than women and non-Caucasians. The preceding list illustrates three important points about the attribution of status based on personal characteristics. First, such characteristics as age, income, occupation, and kinship affect status. Second, for any given individual, status will be conferred according to his own set of values, as evidenced by those who would assert that a white male bank teller has greater status than a black female bank teller. Finally, when an individual and a group agree on the bases of status, it demonstrates a common value system or culture. That is, within particular groups or cultures, there is usually agreement on granting status. In sum, regardless of the personal characteristic which caused an individual to be attributed with status, when it is conferred he will become a valid information source, and the person who conferred it will become susceptible to influence by that source.

Spatial Relations. "Leaders always sit at the head of a table." This common belief reflects the fact that "for Americans the spatial positions of *above* and *in front of* clearly imply superiority of status" (Brown, 1965, p. 78). The fact that judges are "elevated to the bench," most cities have a "Nob Hill," generals enter buildings ahead of lieutenants, and that office size is a touchy subject among executives is no accident. People consistently make judgments of status on the basis of spatial relations; people higher than, in front of, and distant from others are generally regarded as having greater status.

Behavior. If you saw one man ordering another to get him a cup of coffee, you would probably conclude that the order-giver had greater status than the order-follower. Many types of behavior are associated with status, and most are related to influence, power, and control. If the use of power leads to perception of status and if status is related to influence, then the use of power should be related to influence. Bandura, Ross, and Ross (1963) designed an ingenious experiment to demonstrate the point that people seen using power are more imitated than others not seen as powerful. Children were observed to have imitated the behavior of a person who had the power to control rewards for certain behaviors rather than the person who received the rewards. Put simply, status is conferred on those whose behavior implies status.

Sentiments. Feeling superior or inferior in relation to another person obviously affects status and thereby the probability of influence. Feelings of superiority or inferiority are generally an inference based on behavior and are asymmetrical; one person is made to feel superior or inferior *in relation* to another. The person who feels inferior will attribute status to the person he feels inferior to and will, therefore, be susceptible to ISI. Intuitively, the sentiments of superiority and inferiority seem related to the variables of self-esteem, self-confidence, differences in perceived competence, and so on, but the research is so skimpy in this area that conclusions cannot yet be drawn.

Symbols. Many symbols of status are well understood by all, but are seldom articulated. For example, the driver of a Mercedes has greater status for most people than the driver of a Chevrolet; the general wears the symbols of his status on his shoulder; the titles "Dr.," "Sir," and "Count" carry greater status than "Mr." Dress is one of the most common everyday symbols of status. In a clever study conducted by Lefkowitz, Blake, and Mouton (1955) designed to assess the impact of dress on influence, a well-dressed individual crossed a busy street against the light, and many people followed. When dressed in shabby clothes, the same person influenced very few people to cross against the light. The well-dressed (high-status) person was a more valid source of information or a better model than the poorly dressed (low-status) model. Another everyday symbol of status for many people was illustrated in Chapter One—big, new cars do not get honked at as often as rusty, old cars.

Again, however, it must be remembered that the symbols just discussed represent status only because most people have common or similar values. For some, a "woodie" carries greater status than a Mercedes; a peasant blouse, greater status than a Cardin original. The attribution of status because of symbols of status is as much a function of the values of the person conferring status as the symbol which caused it to be conferred. The preceding fact may be called "a receiver orientation to status" and is consistent with the receiver orientation stressed throughout this book.

Attraction

People are more frequently influenced by people they like than by people they do not like. Discussions of why we are attracted to people range from Dale Carnegie's very successful *How to Win Friends and Influence People* to Aristotle's *Rhetoric*. On the basis of much research, however, we can conclude that we are attracted to people, and therefore influenced by them, if they are perceived as any, some, or all of the following: competent, physically attractive, similar to ourselves, possess such admirable qualities as loyalty and honesty, or like us in return. Research into the nature and operation of impression formation and attraction is far too massive to review here. We should note again, however, that what constitutes physical attractiveness, for example, is a function of the individual perceiver; some men are "leg men," whereas others are attracted by large bustlines (a receiver orientation to sexual attraction?). In sum, an attractive, rather than an unattractive, model serves greater informational utility for those who regard him as attractive.

In summary, the relationship between influencer and the person influenced has great impact on ISI. Anonymity decreases the probability of ISI, whereas the attribution of status or attraction increases the probability of ISI. This research is not sufficiently advanced to allow us to resolve the apparent contradiction we have seen in these data. For example, status is conferred because of differences, whereas attraction is frequently perceived due to similarities. Apparently, it would be difficult to be both similar and different, but the research does not suggest which is superior. Nevertheless, either leads to increased probability of ISI. These are going to be important areas of research in future years.

SITUATIONAL FACTORS

Many factors of the specific situation affect an individual's susceptibility to influence. For example, what would your reaction be if a friend indicated that he was going to wear only a swimsuit to a dance you were planning to attend? Would you also wear only a swimsuit? Probably not. What if a second friend indicated that he, too, was going to wear a swimsuit? A third? A fourth? Though there is some dispute (Gerard, Wilhelmy, and Conolley, 1968), research demonstrates that conformity increases with the number of sources of information up to the point of four sources. Beyond that, the probability of influence levels out. Therefore, we might predict that if four of your friends independently indicated that they were going to wear swimsuits to a party, you would either wear a swimsuit also or, at least, wear one under your normal attire so that you could save face if, indeed, everyone was clad briefly.

The influence of sheer numbers of opinions, judgments, or behaviors is probably mediated by the reduction in the level of confidence an individual has in his own judgment, attitude, or behavior and a strong motive to save face. As more people provide information which differs from what an individual thinks is correct or appropriate, his confidence in himself is reduced, his uncertainty increased, his information dependence increased, and therefore his susceptibility to influence is increased. Additionally, as more people agree on a given behavior, attitude, or judgment, the greater the probable identifiability of nonconformity. The greater the publicness or identifiability of your behavior, the stronger the drive to save face and, thus, the susceptibility to influence. The findings about the probability of intervention in an emergency with a large number of people confirm this impact of sheer number; the more people you observe doing nothing in an apparent emergency situation, the lower the probability that you will intervene.

The consistency or unanimity of available information will also affect an individual's susceptibility to ISI. If you are involved in a discussion with four other individuals and all four indicate they think Professor Jones is a "dummie," you will probably agree publicly more frequently than if three indicate they think the professor is a bore and one thinks he is pretty good. Nonconformity to a unanimous majority of opinion is more public and more potentially damaging to face than nonconformity to a nonunanimous decision. For instance, that swimsuit you wore to the dance would probably have been left home if, after your four friends indicated they were going to wear swimsuits, another friend indicated he was going to wear slacks and a dashiki. Unanimous information sources are more influential than nonunanimous ones. Thus, both the number and the consistency of available information sources affect the probability of ISI (Britt, 1971).

The characteristics of the task or decision also affect the probability of ISI. As the *difficulty* of the decision or task, the *ambiguity* of the task, or the *similarity of the judgment alternatives* increase, the uncertainty felt by an individual increases and, as noted previously, information dependence, motivation to save face, and susceptibility to influence all increase. Would your uncertainty be greater in deciding between a free Ford and a free Chevrolet or if given the option of choosing between a Chevrolet and a Ferrari? Most people would need little information in making the latter decision but would need at least some information if given the former decision to make. That need for information translates into susceptibility to ISI. Simple decisions or tasks foster increased self-reliance, reduced information dependence, and decreased probability of ISI.

Susceptibility to influence is affected by characteristics of the observed behavior as well. Behavior which is observed to result in rewards is, obviously, more often used by observers in determining their own behavior than is behavior which results in punishment. Conversely, in numerous studies subjects have been shown to reduce certain types of behavior merely by observing another person being punished for that behavior (Bandura, 1965; Crooks, 1967; Walters, Parke, and Cane, 1965). How many people jaywalk after seeing a jaywalker get hit by a truck? Don't you slow down, at least for a few miles, after you see an auto accident on the freeway?

Behavior which is novel is, at least in the short term, more often influential than usual or common types of behavior. Brown noted that "for short-term learning the behavior need only be novel and attended to. Perhaps any unexpected action that we notice is learned and retained for a short time; novelty is information, and there is an appetite for information in the human species" (1965, p. 399).

Apparently, in terms of solely situational factors, maximum ISI occurs when a group of four or more information sources provide unanimous novel information and when they are seen as being rewarded for their behavior, attitude, or judgment.

CULTURAL FACTORS

The role of culture in ISI is largely a negative one. For instance, people who violate culturally acceptable patterns of behavior (e.g., picking your nose or indiscriminantely scratching yourself in public) lose face, status, attractiveness, and, probably, friends. In short, they lose their utility as information sources or models and are less influential.

A few tentative conclusions about cultural effects on ISI are found in the research literature. For example, some believe (Brown, 1965, pp. 698–702) that groups arrive at extreme decisions, either risky or cautious, in part because our culture values risk or caution in certain circumstances. Individuals who want to have positive traits associated with them and desire to maintain self-image endorse extreme decisions in a group that they would not in private, because they perceive that extremity is valued by others. This may be called the "Audie Murphy syndrome."

Others contend that our culture confers greater positive rewards on individuals for modeling or being influenced by men than by women. This effect of culture is demonstrated by the fact that small children will imitate equally the behavior of both sexes, but by the time they grow up, men are more persuasive than women, and women are more susceptible to influence than men. If this is indeed the case, the women's liberation movement is both correct in its charges of culturally based discrimination and has the difficult task of changing the whole culture rather than merely individuals.

Finally, some researchers argue that conformity and nonconformity are themselves culturally valued in certain, but as yet unspecified, situations. If true, it would mean that certain types of situations would predispose individuals to be either susceptible or resistant to influence. The impact of culture on influence is pervasive, but not understood. When does a description like "company man" cease to be laudatory and become derogatory? When is the American mythical hero, "independent man," congratulated for his independence or called a nonconformist kook? These are all issues requiring future research investigation.

BIOLOGICAL FACTORS

Several demographic or biologic factors have been related to the operation of ISI. All but the most tentative of conclusions, however, are extremely tenuous in this area. For example, probably because of the relationship between age and perceived status, research supports the proposition that older persons are generally more influential than younger ones. Conversely, young people are more susceptible to influence than are their elders (the slavish and sometimes cruel conformity exhibited in junior high schools observationally supports this conclusion).

Some research suggests that, as noted in the preceding section, men are more influential than women (Nicholas, McCarter, and Heckel, 1971) and women are more susceptible to influence than men (Sistrunk, 1971). This research, however, has been plagued by an experimental bugaboo called "treatment bias." The problem has been that the research involved sex-linked topics, e.g., women were more often persuaded than men on such topics as economics and geometry, and men were more persuasive than women in arguing that the World Bank needs a change of policy (Sistrunk and McDavid, 1971).

Some evidence indicates that both blacks and whites are more influenced by whites than by blacks (Sistrunk, 1971). Again, this conclusion must be tempered by a consideration of the changing social climate and the possibility of sampling and research errors in the research which suggests it.

Finally, there is some research suggesting that first-borns are more susceptible to ISI than later-borns (Schacter, 1959). Schacter found that anxiety and affiliation needs were related for first-borns but not later-borns. Thus, as the need for affiliation is related to ISI, one can hold that first-borns are more susceptible to ISI.

SUMMARY

Informational social influence is a nonmanipulative type of influence in which one individual uses the information provided by another to assist in the determination of his own thought, attitude, or behavior. The probability of ISI is a function of information dependence, desire to save face, and situational uncertainty. These three factors, and therefore ISI, are affected by numerous psychological, sociological, situational, cultural, and biological variables.

Psychological Factors

1. *Intelligence.* High-intelligence individuals are less susceptible to ISI than low-intelligence individuals.

2. *Self-esteem.* Persons with high self-esteem are less susceptible to ISI than persons with low self-esteem.

3. *Task-specific self-esteem.* Persons with high task-specific
   self-esteem are less susceptible to ISI than persons with low
   task-specific self-esteem.

4. *Authoritarianism.* High-authoritarians are more susceptible to ISI from "authorities" than are low-authoritarians.

5. *Acquiescence.* Persons with a highly submissive personality
   are more susceptible to ISI than are persons low in that
   personality characteristic.

6. *Anxiety.* Highly anxious persons are more susceptible to
   ISI than are low-anxious persons.

7. *Commitment.* Individuals who are committed to a position
   are less susceptible to ISI than are persons who are not
   committed.

8. *Ego-involvement.* Highly ego-involved persons are less susceptible to ISI than are low-ego-involved persons.

9. *Achievement need.* Individuals with high achievement
   need are more susceptible to ISI than are those with low
   achievement need.

10. *Affiliation need.* Those with high affiliation motives are
    more susceptible to ISI than are those with weak affiliation
    motives.

11. *Social approval need.* Those with a high need for social
    approval are more susceptible to ISI than are those with a
    low need for social approval.

Sociological Factors

1. *Anonymity.* Anonymity reduces susceptibility to ISI.

2. *Status.* Large status differentials result in higher probability of ISI than small status differentials. Status is determined
   by several factors—personal characteristics, spatial relations, behavior, sentiment, and symbols of status.

3. *Attraction.* Attraction to a model increases the probability

of ISI. Attraction is a function of numerous factors—competence, physical attractiveness, similarity, possession of admirable qualities, reciprocation of attraction.

Situational Factors

1. *Size.* The probability of ISI increases with the size of the information pool, up to four, where it levels off.

2. *Unanimity.* Unanimous information pools are more influential than nonunanimous ones.

3. *Ambiguity.* As task ambiguity and difficulty increase, the probability of ISI increases.

4. *Reward.* Rewarded behavior is more influential than nonrewarded or punished behavior.

5. *Novelty.* Novel behavior is more influential than usual or common behavior.

Cultural Factors (tentative and incomplete)

1. *Norms.* Violations of culturally prescribed behavior reduce the probability of ISI.

2. *Sex.* Men are more influential than women; women are more susceptible to influence than men.

3. *Value.*
   a) Conformity and nonconformity are situationally valued.
   b) Risk and caution are situationally valued.

Biological Factors (tentative and incomplete)

1. *Age.* Young people are more susceptible to influence than are older persons; older persons are more influential than young people.

2. *Sex.* Men are more influential than women; women are more susceptible to ISI than are men.

3. *Race.* Whites are more influential than blacks.

4. *Birth order.* First-borns are more susceptible to ISI than are later-borns.

Chapter Three

Normative Social Influence: Outcome Control

Clyde, the student you met in Chapter One, went to work as a construction worker the summer following his sophomore year. His hair was shoulder length, and his hard hat did not have an American flag decal. The crew he worked with questioned both the sexual orientation and the political leanings of "long-haired hippies." They chided Clyde about his hair at every opportunity, avoided any social encounters with him, and never invited him to join them in "hoisting a few" after work. Clyde did not mind this treatment at first, but as the summer wore on he began to feel badly about being rejected by his co-workers. Clyde decided to put an American flag decal on his hard hat. The sarcastic taunting was immediately reduced, but still no significant social advances were made. Finally, Clyde cut his hair. He was quickly accepted, invited to take lunch with the crew, asked to after-work drinking parties, and in the ultimate gesture of friendliness, he was invited to join the bowling league.

Why did Clyde cut his hair? Did he "give in"? Have you ever "given in" in similar circumstances? What did you get in return?

The social influence Clyde experienced was normative social influence (NSI)—Clyde complied with others' imposition of norms or expected patterns of behavior in order to gain something he valued. More specifically, the work crew made known their expectations about hair length and provided social rewards or punishments for meeting or failing to meet those expectations. In short, the work crew had control of an important resource that Clyde wanted, namely, social acceptance. This type of NSI is called *outcome control.*

THE NATURE OF OUTCOME CONTROL NSI

NSI based on outcome control is manipulative in that one or more individuals consciously attempt to affect one or more other individuals. Jones and Gerard (1967) defined outcome control as "one person's ability to determine directly the outcomes (rewards and punishments) of another, and therefore to exert influence over his behavior" (p. 716). In order to determine another's outcomes, the person exerting influence must control the other's attainment of valued goals; that is, he must have power. The recipient of outcome control attempts is influenced because he behaves in ways that will induce others to reward rather than punish him. The person influenced views the exchange as *instrumental;* he complies with expectations of another *in order to* achieve certain goals or rewards. Schein *et al.* (1961) described the extreme example of outcome control that took place in the Communists' "brainwashing" campaigns in Korea as the obvious use of rewards and punishments to induce change in the prisoners. The captors controlled everything that happened to the prisoners and thereby coerced behavioral and psychological modification. This description of the process of outcome control suggests that a type of dependency between influencer and the person influenced is a necessary condition for outcome control to occur. Specifically, outcome control NSI relies on *effect dependence.*

Effect Dependence

Effect dependence is a type of social dependence in which "one person relies on another for the direct satisfaction of needs. The other person is, then, in a position to provide gratifying effects" (Jones and Gerard, 1967, p. 711). The work crew was, for instance, in a position to provide Clyde with social acceptance. You are effect dependent on your professors for course grades, as well as on your friends for a feeling of social approval and acceptance. The degree to which we are dependent on others to achieve desired goals was reviewed by Aronson (1972): "Parents have the power to praise, give love, provide cookies, scream, give spankings, withhold allowances, and so on; teachers have the power to paste gold stars on our foreheads or flunk us out of college; and employers have the power to praise, promote, humiliate, or discharge us" (pp. 31–32).

This ubiquitous form of interpersonal dependence begins, as information dependence, at birth. The human infant has a great many needs he simply cannot satisfy for himself, such as food, shelter, and love. Therefore, he must depend on other people to provide these outcomes. As the child grows he continues to rely on others for attainment of goals. This effect dependence on others continues throughout life and, if a person values or wants a "nice" funeral, even after. This continuing effect dependence during a child's socialization has two important consequences:

1. The child internalizes many norms about beliefs, attitudes, and behaviors for which he has been consistently rewarded or punished. That is, many norms direct a child's behaviors without the administration of consequent rewards or punishments, because of prior learning (e.g., "You must wash your hands before eating" or "Don't draw on the walls").

2. The child learns that the attainment of many goals (e.g., love, money, praise, and approval) can be achieved only through the mediation of another person. The child recognizes his effect dependence on others.

The first result of socialization, the internalization of norms, is largely responsible for the effectiveness of social influence based on *cue control,* the topic of the next chapter. The second consequence, the recognition of one's own effect dependence, is the basis of outcome control NSI.

In sum, the term "effect dependence" describes a relationship between individuals in which one recognizes that he is dependent on another for the attainment of certain desired goals and is, therefore, susceptible to outcome control NSI. For example, if you desire respect, you cannot, by definition, provide that goal for yourself. Further, you know that most people do not give away their respect. Therefore, to get respect you may have to think or behave in ways that will cause the other person to provide his respect. Your effect dependence would make you susceptible to outcome control influence or manipulation. Let's summarize the discussion to this point. Outcome control NSI occurs when one person or a group of people impose expectations on another individual or group of individuals. The person influenced complies with the expectation because he is effect dependent on the influencer for some desired goal. It is a trade: compliance for something the target desires. The crucial question posed by the social reality of effect dependence is: What are the outcomes people want that others control? or What resources can others control in order to exercise influence over those who want them? (Before reading on, try to list the things, relationships, feelings, or states you want that can come only from others.)

Valued Goals

A little thought reveals that the list of desired goals is a virtually endless catalog. No list could be exhaustive. Further, the list would differ from individual to individual; some people want to be leaders and cannot without willing followers, and others want to be followers but need someone to follow. The diversity of goals people want is illustrated by the following examples:

- Earlier in this chapter Clyde wanted and ultimately obtained *social acceptance.*

- Gewirtz and Baer (1958) found that nursery school children desired *social contact* and were very susceptible to influence when it was withheld.

- A recent bribery trial demonstrated that wealthy prisoners wanted and paid for *"favors"* and *physical comfort.*

- The deference employees pay their employers illustrates a common desire for *promotions* or *pay raises.*

- The sales of gas-gobbling, ecologically damaging luxury cars stand as evidence of a pervasive desire by some for *status.*

- The amount of unpaid overtime new employees often work may be the result of a desire for *praise* from superiors.

And the list goes on, and on, and on.

People want many things that can be provided only by other people. One way of identifying and classifying things people want was provided by Maslow (1954). He theorized that people's needs and desires are organized in a hierarchy and that needs lower on the hierarchy must be satisfied before the higher needs become salient in directing behavior. The five levels of need are:

1. Physical needs: hunger, thirst, sex, avoidance of pain, etc.
2. Safety needs: orderliness, familiarity, predictability, etc.

3. Social needs: love, affection, belonging, etc.

4. Ego needs: respect, prestige, status, attention, approval, etc.

5. Self-fulfillment needs: "A musician must make music, an artist must paint, a poet must write if he is ultimately to be put at peace with himself. What a man *can* be he *must be*" (Maslow, p. 91).

Under most circumstances (except those rare cases such as those experienced by P.O.W.'s) the physical and safety needs of adults in our culture are satisfactorily met. Therefore, the social, ego, and self-fulfillment needs direct behavior, and satisfaction of those needs can come only from other people. Outcome control NSI is, therefore, generally based on the control of the outcomes or resources associated with one of the three higher-order needs.

We didn't answer the initial question as to all the goals people desire. Nevertheless, it was noted that: (1) individuals desire many things; (2) specific valued goals or states are individually determined; (3) the attainment of desired goals and avoidance of undesirable ones directs behavior; and (4) the most important outcomes manipulated in outcome control NSI are associated with social, ego, or self-fulfillment needs. Outcome control occurs when a potential influencer (1) correctly identifies another's likes and dislikes, needs, or fears and (2) is in a position to control the other's attainment of those goals.

Let's look at two examples of attempted outcome control. In the first, the influencer correctly identified goals and was in a position to control the other's attainment. In the second, the influencer incorrectly identified valued goals and, despite being in a position to control, didn't influence as he had hoped.

Schein *et al.* (1961) illustrated the importance of identifying those goals an individual considers desirable or undesirable in the operation of the Communist brainwashing techniques in North Korea: "In a well-run reform prison, the authorities made adequate diagnosis of what would constitute significant rewards and punishments for a prisoner (or used trial and error to determine it), and, insofar as possible, organized the prison in such a manner as to maximize the punishment for not confessing or changing attitudes while maximizing the rewards for confession and change."* Once it was known that a given prisoner valued social contact with peers more than anything else, isolation was used as the most effective punishment, and contact with fellow prisoners was used as a reward. For another, isolation from peers was valued because he felt guilty for having "confessed." For all of them, the removal of chains and manacles was rewarding, and their return was punishment. The control of these valued goals was one of the major means of securing "confessions" and ideological conversion in "coercive persuasion."

The impact of incorrect identification of what a person values can be illustrated by an incident in my own experience. While serving in the Air National Guard to avoid the draft, I quickly reached the rank of sergeant. This position was low enough to have few responsibilities, but high enough to avoid "dirty duty." For the military, it was comfortable. The officers incorrectly concluded that I wanted a promotion and occasionally offered a promotion as an incentive for various tasks. Not wanting the additional responsibility associated with promotion, the "incentive" functioned exactly the opposite from the officers' intention: every time the "reward" was offered for a good job, I intentionally "botched" the job. My discharge was as welcomed by the military as it was by me.

AN ECONOMIC EXCHANGE MODEL OF OUTCOME CONTROL NSI

Outcome control has been characterized as a manipulative form of social influence, as an exchange in which one person obtains something he values for his compliance with another's expectations, which the influencer values. This characterization suggests that influence based on outcome control is not unlike an economic exchange in which a buyer obtains something he values only by paying the seller's price. For example, Clyde's

---

*E. H. Schein, I. Schneier, and C. H. Barker, *Coercive Persuasion: A Socio-Psychological Analysis of the "Brainwashing" of American Civilian Prisoners by the Chinese Communists,* New York: Norton, 1961, p. 181. Reprinted by permission.

decision to cut his hair for expected social acceptance is similar
to the decision a consumer makes when he decides that a particular color television set is worth $350. The economic exchange
analogue or explanation for interpersonal influence has been
suggested by many theorists (Blau, 1964; Homans, 1961; Nord,
1969; Thibaut and Kelley, 1959).

An economic exchange model of social influence relies on
the correspondence of certain psychological and economic constructs. That is, economic exchanges have been described and
predicted on the basis of the relationships between such constructs as "commodity," "cost," "price," and "profit." Social
exchange theorists have supplied psychological interpretations
of these concepts in an attempt to describe and predict social
influence exchanges. An examination of the psychological interpretations of these economic concepts is necessary in order
to understand a simplified exchange model of social influence.

Typical economic analysis focuses on the exchange of economic commodities: money and product. The social exchange
theorists' view is that social influence can be similarly characterized as an exchange of compliance and reward (e.g., Clyde
complied with the expectations of others and was rewarded
with social acceptance). Similarly, the "price" in both economic
and social exchanges is the minimal amount of money or compliance a seller will accept in trade for his product or reward.
Conversely, the "cost" is the measure of what must be given up,
either money or compliance, to obtain the commodity desired,
whether product or reward. Finally, the "profit" or "loss" is
simply the determination by each individual involved in an
exchange of the rewards minus the costs. Homans (1961, p. 62)
described the role of the profit motive in social exchanges in this
way: "The open secret of human exchange is to give the other
man behavior that is more valuable to him than it is costly to
you and to get from him behavior that is more valuable to you
than it is costly to him."

Finally, social rewards and compliance can function as
credits and investments in the economic sense. For example,
Jones (1964) has found that the social tactic of *ingratiation* is

really an attempt to provide another person with enough social approval so that the other person "owes" him something, whether it be reciprocated social approval, a favorable word in the right place, respect, or whatever. Similarly, Hollander (1958) introduced the concept of *idiosyncrasy credit*, which postulates that a person who consistently complies and thereby gains social approval and/or status can, occasionally, "cash in" on that prior approval and not comply with a group or other powerful member. Your own experience of punishing some people for given behavior while forgiving the same behavior by others may illustrate the operation of idiosyncrasy credits. Berne (1964) discussed the role of "strokes," social rewards, in *Games People Play.* In everyday exchanges, for example, we return a "stroke" for a "stroke": "Hi"/"Hi"; or "Hi"/"Hi"/"You sure look good today"/"So do you." One never wants to leave an exchange "owing" more strokes than can reasonably be repaid. In sum, the economic concepts of "credit" and "investment" also have psychological analogues.

Before we go on to demonstrate the utility of the psychological explanations of the terms just presented, one assumption about the economic exchange model must be made explicit. This notion of social exchange is based on the hedonistic assumption of man: people are motivated to maximize rewards and minimize costs in social situations. We do not intend to get into the philosophical discussion surrounding this assumption, but its recognition is important. The validity of the hedonistic assumption can never be put to adequate empirical test and must, therefore, be accepted or rejected on the basis of faith or personal experience. In your attempt to wrestle with this issue, you may find it helpful to ask yourself whether you have ever observed, in yourself or others, behavior which violates this assumption. (*Note:* Be careful you don't impose *your* hierarchy of values on another's behavior. Behavior you might not think of as "profitable," such as becoming a cloistered monk or getting arrested for some obscure cause, may be profitable and consistent with the hedonistic assumption for the individual who performed the questionable act.) Now let's use the economic model to look at two social situations.

An analysis of Clyde's decision to put an American flag decal on his helmet and cut his hair demonstrates the utility of the economic exchange model. What does the ledger look like for Clyde's act of compliance? (Knowing Clyde well, as I do, I have assigned mythical numbers representing Clyde's subjective assessment of the rewards and costs for purposes of illustration.)

Description	*Illustrative Value*
1. Clyde wanted social acceptance (reward).	+5
2. The work crew controlled whether or not Clyde received social acceptance and indicated what he had to do to get it—cut his hair (cost).	−3
3. Thus, the profit involved in compliance was equal to Clyde's personal evaluation of his potential rewards minus his costs.	Profit = 5−3 = +2

However, there is also a balance sheet for noncompliance:

Description	*Illustrative Value*
1. Clyde endured social rejection for noncompliance.	−5
2. The rewards for noncompliance included	
a) keeping his hair and	+3
b) any other social acceptance Clyde gained from others outside the work crew by keeping his hair long.	+1
3. Thus, the loss for noncompliance was equal to the rewards minus the costs of noncompliance.	Loss = −5 +3 +1 = −1

We can conclude, on the basis of observed behavior, that Clyde decided that the outcome for noncompliance was a loss, whereas the outcome for compliance was a profit. More specifically, the probability of Clyde's compliance was approximately equal to the profit associated with compliance (+2) minus the loss associated with noncompliance (–1). Thus, the mythical figures clearly favor compliance.

Obviously, given similar circumstances, others may have made different subjective assessments of the value of the cost and reward contingencies associated with compliance and noncompliance, and their behavior would be different. Note, for example, what happens to Clyde's ledger if the social acceptance he gets from groups outside the work crew because of his long hair was worth +5 to Clyde. He would not have complied, as the outcome for compliance would have been less profitable than the outcome for noncompliance. Try to use this economic model to predict your own behavior in Clyde's situation.

The research in coalition formation also demonstrates "economic decision-making." For example, if three small boys want a box of candy that costs five cents, and no one boy had enough money to buy it by himself, a coalition will be formed. If John has two cents, Pete has three cents, and Sam has four cents, which two boys do you think would go together and buy the candy? Research shows that John (2¢) and Pete (3¢) will buy the candy (Gamson, 1964). This situation provides the greatest reward contingency for John and Pete, for John will get 2/5 of the yield, and Pete will get 3/5. If Pete (3¢) had joined with Sam (4¢), he would have got only 3/7 of the yield; if John (2¢) had joined with Sam (4¢) he would have got only 2/6 of the candy. John (2¢), the weakest, or poorest, of the three, is really the strongest in that both of the others wanted to join with him because it would have been more profitable than joining each other. Thus, as has been confirmed repeatedly, the weakest member is truly in the best bargaining position in the process of coalition formation. All of this research is based on and supports the economic exchange model of behavior.

Many types of interpersonal behavior, in addition to Clyde's monumental case of hair-cutting, have been found amenable to this form of analysis. The variety of social influence phenomena susceptible to this type of analysis and explanation includes bargaining, conflict negotiation, leadership, social power, coalition formation, group decision-making, "brain-washing," and conformity. Therefore, the remainder of this chapter will explore these research areas to discover the psychological, sociological, situational, cultural, and biological factors that affect the cost-reward contingencies involved in the operation of outcome control NSI.

PSYCHOLOGICAL FACTORS

If a researcher gave you and a friend the Marlow-Crowne Social Desirability test, he could determine which of you had the greater need for social approval. Assume for a moment that you have a relatively low need for social approval, whereas your friend's need for social approval is relatively strong. Which of you would be more likely to comply when offered social approval in exchange for compliance? Both intuition and research suggest that your friend would be influenced by the potential reward of social approval more than you. This example illustrates that the personality and psychological characteristics of the participants in social exchanges frequently result in individual differences in response to similar situations.

A variety of psychological factors have been demonstrated to affect the operation of outcome control NSI. The known effects of these factors on the influence process under consideration can be organized as they relate to the following propositions:

1. The less costly it is to comply with influence attempts, the more likely compliance will result.

2. The more rewarding it is to comply with influence attempts, the more likely compliance will result.

Hence, we will examine the individual differences that affect the subjective assessment of the costs and rewards of compliance.

The Costs of Compliance

Individuals with high self-esteem regard the acceptance of influence as more costly to themselves than do individuals of low self-esteem. Similarly, those persons with high self-confidence view compliance as more costly than do those of low self-confidence. If these two propositions concerning the relative perception of the costs of compliance are accurate, people with high self-esteem or self-confidence ought to be less susceptible to influence than persons low in either characteristic in similar outcome control situations. The research supports this conclusion (Crowne and Leverant, 1963; Kogan and Wallach, 1967; Samelson, 1957). Similarly, those of low self-perceived status apparently lose less and, therefore, comply more with influence attempts than do individuals who perceive themselves as having high status (Back and Davis, 1965; Jones, Gergen, and Jones, 1963; Menzel, 1957). Is it any wonder that juvenile delinquents, who typically have low evaluations of themselves, are so easily manipulated by the social pressure of their peers (Mischel, 1961)?

The psychological factors of ego-involvement and commitment affect the subjective assessment of the cost of compliance in similar ways. Consider, for instance, how reactions might differ in the following situations. You have decided to go to a rock concert on the weekend, told many friends of your plans, and rejected an invitation to a party. Then, a number of friends say, "What a dumb waste of money, those concerts are just an overpriced attempt to rip-off teenagers!" Would you go to the concert and risk the disapproval of your friends? What if you had made the decision to go, but had not yet purchased your tickets, told anyone, or rejected the party invitation and then heard your friends' comments when you discussed your intentions? In the first case, compliance with your friends' obvious expectations would be both financially and personally costly because of the extent of your commitments. In the latter case, on the other hand, you could accept your friends' influence attempts with little costs incurred. In sum, the probability of influence is lower when the target of influence is highly committed than when he is not so committed. Similar reasoning leads one to the conclusion that the more ego-involved an individual is, the less likely is successful influence by others. Specifically, when a person is ego-involved in a topic, his attitude about that topic is important to him, and he uses that attitude as an "anchor" for making other judgments. Therefore, accepting influence on any given topic is more costly, as the person is more ego-involved in his attitude on that topic. It would obviously be more costly for the president of an ecology club to be persuaded to endorse a housing development than it would be for a rank-and-file member who, presumably, is not as ego-involved in conservation. Research into the operation of both of these factors confirms that acceptance of influence is perceived as more costly and is, therefore, less likely when the target person is highly committed or highly ego-involved (Carment, 1961; Gerard, 1964; Zimbardo, 1960).

If you will recall the discussion from Chapter Two of the personality trait of authoritarianism you will note that those high in this characteristic continually refer and defer to authorities in social situations. It is, therefore, not surprising to find that the research suggests the conclusion that high-authoritarians are more susceptible to outcome control from those they regard as "authorities" than are low-authoritarians (Centers, Shomer, and Rodrigues, 1970). Similarly, when a high-status source attempts to exert influence over a person who is highly dogmatic, it will likely be more successful than if the target were a low-dogmatic (Croner and Willis, 1961). For both authoritarians and dogmatics, the costs of compliance to authorities are low and influence more probable than for low-authoritarians and dogmatics. This may be explained, in part, by the fact that both personality characteristics involve an investment and faith in the power structure of the status quo, and acceptance of influence is, in a sense, rewarding in that it maintains power relationships.

Another way to view the social exchange involved in outcome control NSI is to focus on the psychological factors that increase the subjective value of the rewards for compliance.

The Rewards For Compliance

A general proposition about the rewards for compliance is suggested by the research: The greater the intensity of need for social rewards, the greater the perceived value of the rewards and the greater the probability of influence based on outcome control of that need. In other words, the more an individual wants something, the more he values its attainment, and the more susceptible he is to influence involving that outcome. For example, earlier we hypothesized that your friend would be more susceptible to influence because of his greater need for social approval. Need strength, according to Schein *et al.* (1961), played a role in the "coercive persuasion" used by the Communists in Korea. The effect of physical deprivation on the prisoners was such as to "make the prisoner sufficiently uncomfortable to want to get out of prison quite badly, and in this sense the prison regimen induced a strong force toward finding *some* solution to his problems. The recognition of needing to make a certain kind of confession as *the* solution might have come much later; but once the recognition came there were strong motives available to make the prisoner go through with it."* In sum, the stronger the need, whether social, physical, safety, ego, or self-fulfillment, the greater the susceptibility to influence (DiVesta and Merwin, 1960).

The needs for approval, affiliation, and status have all been empirically investigated, and the suggested relationship has been consistently maintained (Becker and Carroll, 1962; Berenda, 1950; Blau, 1960; Erickson, 1962; Smith and Flenning, 1971; Zipf, 1960). The effects of the need for independence have also been researched, and consistent with the general proposition just presented, people with a strong need for independence were found to be less susceptible to influence than those with a weak need for independence (Zipf, 1960).

McDavid (1959) examined the effects of being "person-oriented" or "task-oriented" on the influence process. He found that subjects who were person-oriented rather than task-oriented were more susceptible to power attempts. However, the effects of this distinction apparently were mediated by need for social approval. McDavid noted that person-oriented individuals have a greater need for social approval and that it was their heightened need that resulted in increased susceptibility to influence.

Need strength to avoid undesirable states is as important to the operation of outcome control influence as need strength to attain desirable states. Janis (1955) found that those with greater fear of social rejection were more susceptible to influence than

---

*Schein, *et al.*, *Coercive Persuasion*, pp. 175–176. Reprinted by permission.

those with low fear of social rejection. Apparently, the effects of anxiety are mediated by this fear of social rejection as well. Specifically, the anxious person typically wants to avoid appearing different from others, fears social rejection, and views compliance as highly rewarding because it facilitates avoiding these undesirable states. Therefore, the highly anxious person places greater value on compliance and is more susceptible to influence than are individuals who are not anxious (Steiner and Vannoy, 1966; Walters and Karal, 1960).

Obviously, the success of an outcome control influence attempt will be, in part, a function of the psychological characteristics of the target person. As will be made increasingly evident, successful intentional influence depends to a great extent on the influencer's analysis of his target and his ability to structure his influence attempt for a particular target.

SOCIOLOGICAL FACTORS

Several aspects of the relationship between the influencer and the person influenced have been researched. Before we discuss these, however, we must recognize that there are two minimal, or basic, social conditions that must exist for outcome control NSI to take place at all—effect dependence and identifiability.

The target of outcome control influence attempts must perceive himself effect dependent on the influencer. Unless he perceives the other person as capable of controlling resources he values, influence will not occur. This minimal condition was recognized by Emerson (1962), who noted that "*power resides implicitly in the other's dependency*" (p. 32). The importance of effect dependence can be easily illustrated. If a fellow student said to you, "Unless you turn in the term paper, I will see that you fail this course," you would probably be little affected. If, on the other hand, the same message came from your professor, it would undoubtedly result in some effect. You are effect dependent on your professor for a course grade, but you are not effect dependent on another student for that grade (unless the professor is effect dependent on that student for something else). Thus, for outcome control NSI to occur, an effect-dependent relationship between influencer and the person influenced must exist.

The second necessary condition for outcome control to take place is identifiability. Unless the target perceives that his behavior can be observed by the influencer, the probability of an exchange, receiving rewards for compliance, is slight. Similarly, unless the influencer has surveillance of the target, punishment for noncompliance is unlikely. The importance of identifiability was illustrated in a study by Festinger (1953) in which factory workers increased their rate of production to the level the supervisor expected *when he was present,* but their production fell off when the supervisor could not observe their performance. The target must be identifiable to the influencer.

When both of these conditions have been met, the resulting social situation is one of power. The bases of power are numerous, and as Jacobson noted (1972), power may be attributed to a person for a variety of reasons:

> He may have personality characteristics that are important in a particular social relationship; he may control wealth or have access to information desired by others. The wielder of power may have physical strength or be able to call upon force from other sources. His resources may consist of certain tasks or general abilities, such as the ability to speak well or to organize people and materials effectively. The ability to provide praise, recognition, or affections, or to punish and minimize opportunities for others, may also be resources."*

In this section we are going to discuss two types or bases of power—actual power and social power. Actual power arises out of the real or imagined control by one person over the rewards and punishments of another. Social power arises from the relationship between influencer and the person influenced. The distinctions between these two types of power will become more clear in the discussion that follows.

---

*W. D. Jacobson, *Power and Interpersonal Relations,* Belmont, Calif.: Wadsworth, 1972, p. 21. Reprinted by permission.

Actual Power

An employer can promote an employee, a teacher can fail a student, parents can spank a child, the wealthy can give money to the poor, a dentist can help a person with a toothache. In each of these examples, one person can control another's attainment of a valued goal or resource, virtually independent of, or in spite of, the other's thought or action. In other words, regardless of what the target feels, thinks, or does, the person controlling the resource can help or hinder in the target person's attainment of goals. This is actual power. The possessor of actual power can easily influence an individual by means of outcome control NSI. The only question in such cases is the target's evaluation of the costs and rewards involved in the exchange. Let's look at one example of the most crude form of power.

When Clyde's brother came up for promotion in a large company, he had to have an interview with the vice-president. During the interview the vice-president, who had complete freedom in choosing the person to be promoted, said that no senior executive in the company was allowed to wear a beard. He also indicated that Clyde's brother was the best-qualified person for the job, but "Unless you are willing to get rid of the beard, no promotion." Simple, bald-faced (no pun intended) power. Clyde's brother debated the relative costs of shaving off his beard against the rewards of promotion. He was promoted two weeks later.

Now, actual power can exist "out there" as a function of the real situation, or it can be imagined. That is, A can actually have power over B, or B can *believe* that A has actual power over him, whether he does or not. It turns out that there is little real difference between actual and imagined or functional power. The question, then, is "Why do people *attribute* actual power to another person?" Another way of asking the same question is "What makes people think another person can actually control their attainment of valued goals or resources?" Individuals attribute actual power to another when the other person is seen as being older, more intelligent, or more competent. If a person talks a lot, attempts influence frequently, or holds a position or title that implies power, he is also seen as powerful.

Finally, if a person is viewed as possessing high status, he is perceived as being powerful. Each of these areas has received a good deal of research, but we will explore each only briefly.

Older people are often perceived to have actual control over the resources (promotion, money, punishment, etc.) valued by younger people. This effect is probably due in part to childhood experiences in which older people, such as siblings, parents, and teachers, were, in fact, more powerful. Perceived power as a function of age was demonstrated in studies by Sutton-Smith and Rosenberg (1968) and Duncker (1938).

People who are seen as more intelligent or more competent are also viewed as powerful in many circumstances (Mulder, Mauk, and Wilke, 1970; Patel and Gordon, 1960; Willis, 1963). Perceived intelligence and competence both result from an unequal distribution of resources, knowledge, and ability. And since power is attributed to those who possess more of a valued resource, competent and intelligent people are attributed with power.

The title or position a person holds may also be the basis for power being attributed to him. This effect was observed in a study by Torrance (1965). He found that among newly formed flight crews, power was distributed according to position: the pilot was more powerful than the navigator, and the navigator was more powerful than the crew. Since actual power is so often associated with title or position, the attribution of actual power because of title or position is natural.

If a person talks a lot or tries to exercise influence frequently, he will often be seen as powerful (French and Snyder, 1959; Gray, Richardson, and Mayhew, 1968; Riecken, 1958). Both activities, influencing and dominating conversation, are frequently observed in persons who are actually powerful. The fact that the observation of either attribute leads to the attribution of power is an understandable association.

Finally, low-status people frequently attribute actual power to high-status persons. As discussed in Chapter Two, there are many bases for the attribution of status (personal characteristics, spatial relations, behavior, etc.) Whatever the reason for the attribution of status, apparently actual power and the ability to influence go along with it.

To conclude this section, whether the actual power of an individual is real or imagined, once the target believes the other person possesses actual power, he becomes susceptible to outcome control NSI.

Social Power

Social power arises out of interpersonal relations. Social power is based primarily on another's control of social and ego needs; the amount of social power A holds over B is a function of the value B places on the social rewards A can offer. Note the emphasis on B's evaluation of the rewards A can offer, not just the evaluation of the rewards per se. This distinction may be made clearer if you place yourself in the following common situation.

When you have the possibility of receiving social approval from a person you like and one you don't like, you obviously would value the social approval from your friend more than that of the other person. One always likes social approval, the reward, but the origin of the social approval determines just how valuable it is. Social power, then, is the power that results because of the target's high evaluation of the rewards provided by a *particular person.*

Since social power arises from that nature of a particular social relationship, the important question is: What social relationships increase the perceived value of rewards and punishments? Generally, the research has concluded that the rewards offered by people we *like* (Hurwitz, Zander, and Hymovitch, 1968), are *attracted to* (Darley, 1966; Jackson and Saltzstein, 1958), or are *similar to* (Linde and Patterson, 1964; Walker and Heyns, 1962) are perceived as more valuable. Similarly, the punishments from people we like, are attracted to, or are similar to are evaluated as more negative. Thus, people involved in these types of social relations have social power. Therefore, when respect, social approval, social rejection or acceptance, liking, and other social or ego needs are traded, social power affects the exchange.

The impact of social power is suggested by yet another area of research. Researchers have found that cohesive groups (groups with a good deal of attraction between members) exercise greater influence over their members than those groups that are not cohesive (Fiedler and Meuwese, 1963). Wouldn't you fear social rejection from a group more if that group was very attractive to you than if it weren't?

Before we conclude this discussion of sociological factors of outcome control, we must consider a limiting condition to the conclusions we've reached. Specifically, just because a person feels effect dependent on another and his behavior is identifiable does not mean necessarily that influence will take place. If the individual can get the same rewards at a lower cost or greater rewards at the same cost somewhere else, the exchange won't take place. Thus, the prediction of outcome control NSI must account for the availability to the target of alternative relationships (Thibaut and Kelley, 1959). The freshman, for example, who wants social acceptance and finds he can get it at a fraternity by adopting the members' life style, may decide he can also get social acceptance by living in a boarding house where his costs, both financial and personal, are not as great. Were it not for the availability of so many alternatives for virtually any type of reward, society would be most Machiavellian; that is, just keep increasing the rewards or punishments, and compliance will ultimately be achieved.

SITUATIONAL FACTORS

The variety of situational variables that has been shown to affect outcome control NSI is staggering and, unfortunately, the results are in a state of disarray. Many of the experiments dealt with variables relating to the proposition that compliance increases as the perceived value of the rewards increases or the perceived value of costs decreases. What kinds of situational factors affect the target's evaluation of rewards and costs?

The amount of deprivation the target has experienced prior to the influence attempt will obviously affect the perception of the worth of the deprived reward (Staats *et al.*, 1972). Gewirtz and Baer (1958) found, for example, that verbal approval was a stronger positive reinforcement for children who had been deprived of social approval than for children satiated with social approval. Similarly, socially mediated rewards are apparently subject to the economic law of diminishing marginal utility. That is, social rewards from a person who gives those rewards away freely are viewed as less valuable than the same rewards from someone more stringent. Thus, both the target's deprivation and the influencer's typical pattern of reward-giving affect the perceived value of rewards and the probability of influence based on those outcomes.

The availability to the target of outside reference groups for goal attainment also affects the perception of the value of rewards and costs (Festinger and Thibaut, 1951). Thus, the more available alternative sources of need satisfaction are to the target, the less likely is outcome control. The psychological economy of this situation can be illustrated by a common example. If you need a particular class for graduation and it is taught only by one extremely demanding professor only once a year, you would be far more likely to comply or "put up with" the difficult requirements of the class than if the class was offered every term by numerous teachers. In the latter situation your options are greater (take it next term, take it from a different teacher, or both), and the perceived cost of staying in Dr. Difficult's class are greater.

The nature of the topic or task also affects the target's perception of the reward-cost contingencies in outcome control. Specifically, as the task becomes more difficult or ambiguous, the perception of the value of the rewards associated with compliance increases because the compliance provides a resolution to a difficult task (Suppes and Krasne, 1961). Similarly, the costs of compliance decline as the difficulty of the task increases, because compliance becomes less obvious. For example, note in Fig. 3–1 that agreement with the erroneous decision of the group in the conformity situation is less obvious in Situation 1 than in Situation 2.

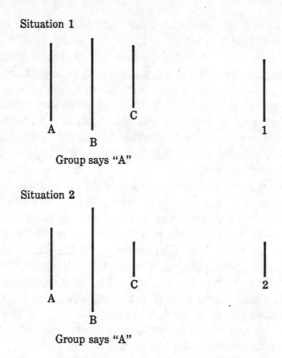

Situation 1

A
B
C
1
Group says "A"

Situation 2

A
B
C
2
Group says "A"

Fig. 3-1 Two conformity situations of differing difficulty.

The target's anticipation of future events will affect the present outcome control attempts. Two expectations of the target have been researched—the possibility of achieving acceptance and the possibility of continuing contact.

Dittes and Kelley (1956) found that a group can exercise greatest control over those who are moderately accepted by the group, but that those who are already accepted or virtually rejected accept very little influence. Individuals already accepted by the group don't need to comply to gain additional acceptance, and those rejected probably perceive little possibility of gaining acceptance *even if* they accept the group's influence. The moderately accepted person, on the other hand, hopes to gain an even better position within the group and assumes that acceptance of influence is the way to achieve it (Becker and Carroll, 1962).

Similarly, if the target thinks he will have or desires to have continuing contact with the influencer, the value of the rewards and the costs of punishment are greater, and compliance is more likely (Rotter, 1966). In short, if a person thinks he will have continuing contact with another person, he views acceptance of influence as an investment in future exchanges. The perception of continuing contact increases the probability of outcome control NSI.

Though the research is still skimpy, it appears that "the total amount of influence effected by a leader (or member) over a member increases with the amount of influence attempted" (French and Snyder, 1959, p. 121). This hypothesis was tested and confirmed by Gray, Richardson, and Mayhew (1968). The apparent explanation for this seemingly illogical hypothesis is that a target's perception of the influencer's status increases as he sees the influencer exercise power, a high-status behavior; the increased status, in turn, increases the value of the rewards mediated by the influencer. Consequently, the increased perception of value associated with the rewards mediated by the influencer increases the probability of influence. Thus, despite the circularity of the proposition, the probability of influence increases as the amount of influence attempted increases.

The probability of successful outcome control NSI is, in part, a function of the specific message employed. All messages involved in outcome control NSI are *contingency messages:* If you do (or don't do) X, I will (or won't do) Y. In terms of the receiver's perceptions, two important questions arise when such messages are received.

1. What is the degree and type of contingency involved?

2. What is the probability of the contingency?

Let's examine the research that relates to each of these questions. Obviously, the contingency message can be either a reward contingency or a punishment contingency. Though there appears to be some situational variance, reward and punishment contingencies are equally effective (Brigante, 1958;

Kipnis, 1958; Wenburg, 1969; Zipf, 1960). That is, outcome control influence based on rewarding for specified behaviors or punishing for specified behaviors are equally effective in inducing compliance to expectations.

The magnitude or value of the reward or punishment involved in the suggested contingency is positively related to acceptance. For example, the probability of influencing you to skip class increases as the monetary reward for doing so increases or monetary punishment for skipping class decreases. What would be the threshold amount of money to induce you to skip class? Four cents? One dollar? Five dollars? Five hundred dollars? Whatever your answer, it appears that five dollars would more likely result in a greater probability for skipping class than would four cents. In sum, the magnitude of the reward or punishment provided by the contingency message is positively related to message acceptance (Dabbs and Leventhal, 1966; Leventhal, Singer, and Jones, 1963; Lindskold, Bonoma, and Tedeschi, 1969; Tedeschi, 1970).

Furthermore, the clarity of the contingency is positively related to compliance. The more obvious the connection between doing X or not doing X and getting a specific reward or punishment, the greater the probability of influence. The statement by a professor, "It might be a good idea to get that paper in by Friday" is not as clear and unambiguous as "If you don't get that paper in by Friday, I will flunk you in this course." The implicit statement of contingency is less obvious and less likely to induce compliance than the very clear and explicit statement of contingency.

Finally, the object of the contingency statement affects the likelihood of influence. At least for punishment contingencies, if the target's refusal to comply results in injury or punishment to a third party ("If you don't get that paper in, I'll flunk your girl friend in this course"), it will be more effective in inducing compliance than if the target himself must bear the punishment for noncompliance (Hornstein, Deutsch, and Benedict, 1966). Could this be why we have seen so many television commercials scaring the hell out of husbands and fathers: "If you don't take Super Vitamin, your wife will be a widow"? Thus, we can tentatively conclude that punishment contingencies involving the target alone are not as effective as those involving a third person the target values.

Tedeschi (1970) noted that "empirical research has established that behavioral compliance to threats is a function of the credibility of threats and the magnitude of punishment associated with threats" (p. 175). Clearly, the target's perception of the influencer's ability to actually carry out the contingency, whether reward or punishment, will affect the target's probability of compliance (Pollard and Mitchell, 1972). For example, Miller and Hewgill (1966) found that high-credible sources were more effective than low-credible sources when they used a high fear-producing message. Undoubtedly, the perceived ability of the low-credibility source to predict or control the completion of a fear contingency is lower than for the high-credible source. The target, simply, must believe that the influencer can actually control or predict the outcomes suggested by the contingency in his message; otherwise, the contingency will be ineffective.

CULTURAL FACTORS

One of the most important factors in the economic analysis of social influence is the "cost" involved in compliance. If compliance were not viewed by its suppliers as costly, providing compliance would not warrant reward—people would give it away, whether or not they received anything in return. The *degree* of cost involved in compliance is apparently a function of many factors, but the basic proposition that compliance is costly is a product of culture. Jones and Jones (1964) found that people who wanted to gain respect from others exhibited only moderate amounts of compliance, because they wanted to avoid appearing "slavishly conforming." Luchins and Luchins (1955) reported that children who did not accept influence frequently reported that they didn't want to look like "copy-cats." Further evidence of the social and personal cost of compliance can be found by analyzing a common stereotype, e.g., in our culture the "yes-man" is a pejorative characterization. In sum, in our culture compliance with others is perceived as costly to self-esteem and respect.

Another impact of culture on the perceived cost of compliance can be found in sex differences. Because of cultural roles and stereotypes, it is apparently less costly for women to comply with influence attempts than it is for men (Endler, 1966; Carrigan and Julian, 1966). Furthermore, consistent with the stereotypic upbringing of women, women are more susceptible to influence when social approval is offered in exchange for compliance.

BIOLOGICAL FACTORS

Numerous studies have demonstrated that the young comply more frequently with influence attempts than do their elders (Iscoe and Williams, 1963; McConnel, 1963; Patel and Gordon, 1960). In terms of the economic model discussed in this chapter, the young seemingly view compliance as less costly than do older persons. That is, young individuals generally perceive fewer alternatives and have lower levels of self-confidence, both of which would result in the young perceiving compliance as less costly.

SUMMARY

NSI based on outcome control is a form of social exchange whereby compliance is traded for something the target values. The operation of outcome control depends on effect dependence, identifiability, and the correct analysis of the desired goals or resources of the target. The "rules" governing this process of social influence are analogous to those involved in economic exchanges. Many factors affect the "economic" decision-making of NSI based on outcome control.

Psychological Factors

1. *Need.* The greater the need felt by the target, the greater the probability of influence trading on need-related resources:
   a) need for *social approval*
   b) need for *affiliation*
   c) need for *status*
   d) need to avoid *undesirable states.*

2. *Self-esteem.* The greater the self-esteem of an individual, the less susceptible he is to influence.

3. *Self-confidence.* The greater the self-confidence of an individual, the less susceptible he is to influence.

4. *Self-perceived status.* The greater the self-perceived status of an individual, the less susceptible he is to influence.

5. *Ego-involvement.* The greater the level of ego-involvement of a person, the less susceptible he is to influence.

6. *Commitment.* The greater the level of commitment by an individual, the less susceptible he is to influence.

7. *Authoritarianism.* The greater the level of authoritarianism of an individual, the more susceptible he is to influence from "authorities."

8. *Dogmatism.* The greater the level of dogmatism of an individual, the more susceptible he is to influence from "authorities."

9. *Need for independence.* The greater the need for independence within an individual, the less susceptible he is to influence.

Sociological Factors

1. *Effect dependence.* Outcome control influence cannot occur without the perceived relationship of effect dependence between influencer and target.

2. *Identifiability.* Outcome control influence cannot occur unless the target and his behavior are under the surveillance of the influencer.

3. *Actual power.* The greater the actual power an influencer possesses, whether real or imagined, the greater the probability of influence.

   a) *Age.* Older people are perceived as more powerful than younger people.

   b) *Intelligence and competence.* Intelligent and competent people are perceived as more powerful than unintelligent or incompetent people.

c) *Title or position.* People who hold positions or titles that imply power are seen as more powerful than those who do not hold such titles or positions.

d) *Communication and influence.* People who dominate communication or attempt influence frequently are seen as more powerful than those who do not communicate or attempt influence frequently.

e) *Status.* High-status persons are seen as more powerful than low-status persons.

4. *Social power.* The greater the social power a person possesses, the greater the probability of influence.

a) *Attraction.* People perceived as attractive have greater social power than those perceived as unattractive.

b) *Liking.* People who are liked have greater social power than people who are disliked.

c) *Similarity.* People who are perceived as similar to the target have greater social power than those perceived as dissimilar.

5. *Alternative relationships.* The greater the number and availability of alternative sources of need satisfaction, the lower the probability of social influence.

Situational Factors

1. *Deprivation.* The greater the deprivation of reward, the greater the probability of influence based on that reward.

2. *Availability of reward.* The greater the ease of obtaining a reward, the lower the probability of influence based on that reward.

3. *Alternative relationships.* The greater the number and availability of alternative sources of need satisfaction, the lower the probability of influence.

4. *Task difficulty and ambiguity.* The greater the difficulty or ambiguity of the task, the greater the probability of influence.

5. *Anticipated acceptance.* The greater the perceived possibility of improving social acceptance, the greater the probability of influence based on social acceptance.

6. *Anticipated future interaction.* The greater the probability of future interaction, the greater the probability of influence.

7. *Influence attempted.* The more influence attempted by a source, the greater the probability of influence in the next instance of attempt.

8. *Types of contingencies.* Reward and punishment messages are probably equally effective.

9. *Magnitude of reward or punishment.* The greater the magnitude of reward or punishment involved in the influence contingency, the greater the probability of influence.

10. *Clarity of message.* The greater the clarity of contingency messages, the more probable is influence.

11. *Probability of contingency.* The greater the probability of the contingency, the greater the probability of influence.

Cultural Factors (tentative and incomplete)

1. *Cost of compliance.* In our culture compliance is viewed as costly to self-esteem and respect.

    a) *Sex.* In our culture, compliance is less costly for women than for men.

Biological Factors (tentative and incomplete)

1. *Age.* The young comply more frequently than do the old.

Chapter Four

Normative Social Influence: Cue Control

Given Clyde's situation, it really was not surprising that he cut his hair. Furthermore, it is not particularly insightful of a teacher to offer a longer recess so her students will be quiet. Exchanges of compliance and rewards or noncompliance and punishments are everyday experiences, and the rules governing these exchanges are implicitly understood by everyone. What is intriguing is that people can influence others to do things *without* providing rewards and punishments. That is, it is a common observation that influence can occur without any form of social exchange. Examine the following instances of noncontingent influence, that is, influence without a deliberate exchange of social goods.

- We tune in on "Plaxton Palace" and find Hortense and Henrietta talking at a party. Hortense is having an affair with Harold, Henrietta's husband, and the topic of conversation turns to adultery. Naturally, Hortense is trying to steer the conversation away from this topic.

  Henrietta: Did you hear that Mary and John are having an affair?

  Hortense: Henrietta, what a beautiful dress!

  Henrietta: Oh, do you really like it? Is this the first you've heard of Mary's fling?

  Hortense: This certainly is a lovely party.

  Henrietta: Yes, the Clapboards always entertain beautifully. You know, if Harold ever began messing around, I'd kill him *and* the girl.

  Hortense: I hear you are going to Aspen this year.

  Henrietta: Oh yes, we love Aspen. Have you ever been there?

  Hortense: No, I haven't. Tell me about it. (Whew!)

- On occasion, when a doctor discovers that his patient has cancer, he does not inform his patient of the illness, on the grounds that if the patient found out, he might behave in ways that would interfere with necessary treatment. The doctor wants to treat the patient, and informing the patient of his illness may call out behavior counterproductive for the patient.

- For many years "Lumpy Crunch" cereal has paid a very ex-famous athlete to say on television that he liked "Lumpy Crunch" cereal. For about the same period of time, "Lumpy Crunch" cereal has been one of the top-selling breakfast products.

- Vance Packard, who popularized and overrated the concern for mass advertising, reported that housewives were once given the same detergent in one of three boxes: a yellow box, a blue box, or a yellow and blue box. The housewives reported that the detergent in the blue box left their clothes dirty, the detergent in the yellow box was too strong, and the detergent in the yellow and blue box was just right.

- "Friends, I come back to my beloved state to talk to you about some issues important to us. We know that the crime rate is rising and that there are those who want to coddle criminals. We know that policemen are murdered almost every day, but many worry about the 'civil rights' of criminals."
  BLAH
  BLAH
  BLAH
  Friends, our fathers, who toiled this beautiful land, did not work so hard so others can tear down the product of their labor. I ask you to send me back to the Senate so I can continue to labor in pursuit of our common goals."

Each of the preceding instances was an example of normative social influence based on *cue control*. Since cue control constitutes such a large proportion of the total amount of influence that takes place every day, we will explore its operation in depth in this chapter.

THE NATURE OF CUE CONTROL NSI

NSI based on cue control operates largely because the receiver, or target of influence, is an active participant in the process. Within each person there are certain dispositions or tendencies that direct behavior when they are made salient, and cue control involves the activation of these dispositions. Jones and Gerard (1967) characterized cue control as "the use of information about previously learned contingencies to trigger certain responses in another. Unlike the case of *outcome control,* the controlling person need not possess resources desired by the other; he need only provide a cue that elicits a habitual response sequence" (p. 710). The notion involved here is that one person provides cues, or stimuli, that are designed to elicit, or arouse, part of another's response repertoire. The person influenced views the influence as *instrumental;* he complies with the activated disposition *in order to* be consistent within himself. I might, for example, influence your opinion of poor Clyde if I could convince you that he called your sister a "hooker." In this case, I do not have to control punishments or rewards; rather, I merely rely on your highly probable reaction to such a malicious characterization of your sister.

Cue control NSI is manipulative in that it involves one person's intentionally attempting to influence another. No specific reward or punishment is mediated by the influencer; rather, the target "monitors himself, as it were, and applies some equivalent of the rewards and punishments that were formerly a part of the reactions of others" (Jones and Gerard, 1967, p. 84). Thus, cue control NSI relies on the elicitation of pre-established dispositions that are intrinsically self-rewarding.

The key to effective cue control is the identification of these "pre-established dispositions" so that they can be made salient to direct behavior. In other words, cue control relies on the arousal of specific dispositions, and such reliance demands a careful examination of these dispositions. Jones and Gerard (1967) noted that "effective presentation of appropriate cues depends in turn on some knowledge of the other's past history and therefore his dispositions" (pp. 535–536). In summary, in the exercise of cue control, knowledge of the target's dispositions is equivalent to power to influence. The examples earlier in this chapter illustrate some common dispositions. Hortense, for instance, relied on the common disposition of people to follow conversational leads when she tried to avoid talking about adultery. The saccharine senator relied on the disposition of people to like other people who are similar to themselves.

Types of Dispositons

A disposition is a relatively enduring characteristic of an individual which directs behavior when it is made salient. A disposition is analogous to an inclination or a tendency. With the exception of the questionable and limited category of innate dispositions or instincts, all dispositions are learned. The dispositions to be considered in this discussion of cue control are internalized cultural norms, well-learned responses, expectations, and attitudes. The role played by the first three of these types of dispositions is not well understood as they relate to influence processes. The last disposition, attitude, has received a great deal of research interest and will receive a correspondingly disproportionate amount of consideration in this chapter. In the following discussion, each of these dispositions will be explored and its relationship to influence processes explained.

Internalized Cultural Norms. A culture is frequently defined as the aggregate of common or shared beliefs, values, and behavior expectations within a community, group, or society. The process of socialization results in each individual's internalizing these common beliefs, values, and behavior expectations. Dispositions are considered internalized or socialization is considered complete when an individual maintains and lives by these dispositions without external control. When a person is socialized, he evaluates his own behavior as it relates to cultural norms. Some call this a "conscience." But the "socialized individual not only learns some of the regularities contained in the cultural map; he is himself bound (constrained) in various ways by the regularities and contributes to them" (Jones and Gerard, 1967, p. 176). Furthermore, he is not even likely to be aware of such constraints, as the process of socialization results in his inability to even perceive alternatives to the expected behaviors. In sum, one important product of the process of socialization is that every member of a culture learns, internalizes, common cultural patterns of thought and action and is constrained by these internalized norms.

An individual's culture imposes itself on an individual by means of roles and their associated norms. People learn the traditional relationships and the behavior expected in these relationships. For example, each individual knows what norms direct such relationships as father and son, husband and wife, driver and pedestrian, student and teacher, leader and member, employer and employee, and so on. Isn't it likely that the internalized norms concerning the roles of brother and sister or sister and sister were, at least in part, responsible for your reaction to Clyde's having called your sister a "hooker"? Your response, in other words, was partly a function of your culturally induced expectations of self in such circumstances.

Another important consequence of the internalization of cultural norms is the simplification of behavioral alternatives in complex social situations. The effort needed in thinking and behaving in a complex social environment can be reduced to the extent that a culture provides "rules of thumb" for behavior. As the proportion of culturally automated decisions increases, the individual is freed to deal with those behavior decisions not covered by cultural rules of thumb. Shor (1972) conducted an interesting field study that demonstrated this simplifying function of cultural norms. He investigated two cities, Boston, Massachusetts, and Lawrence, Kansas, and found that the cities had developed different norms about driving behavior. In Boston the rule of thumb apparently is that every driver behaves competitively; he is out for himself and everyone knows it. The shared expectations, or norms, in Lawrence, on the other hand, "require and expect that every driver will first show courtesy to others before taking his own advantage" (Shor, 1972, p. 320). Shor noted that "both systems work efficiently for their respective traffic conditions. In urban Boston less effort is required in the long run when everyone acts competitively. In rural Lawrence less effort is required in the long run when everyone acts courteously" (p. 320). The norms made certain behavior decisions automatic and reduced the complexity of the driving situation. The norms are dysfunctional or work to the detriment of a person, however, when they do not match the situation, such as when a Bostonian is in Lawrence.

Each individual has numerous dispositions (inclinations or tendencies) to act and think in specified ways in particular circumstances. Many dispositions occur as the result of the internalization of cultural norms. The exercise of cue control, therefore, is the provision of cues which make salient the culturally automated responses desired. Try to determine how much of your own behavior is culturally automated. (Beware you do not underplay the effects of culture merely because your socialization is so complete that you do not immediately perceive any real alternatives to the culturally dictated behavior.)

Well-Learned Responses. Cue control often relies on an internal disposition or tendency that is the result of extensive learning experiences of an individual. Just as a culture induces acceptance by almost all its members of certain standards of thought and action, an individual's personal experience induces the internalization of a variety of well-learned responses to specific situations. Whether the learning occurred as the result of instrumental or classical conditioning, the end result is an association between situation and response. For example, a child's language environment may bias him toward certain evaluative dispositions. When a child hears such negatively connoted words and phrases as "blackmail," "black-listed," "black market," "black-balled," "black-hearted," "black sheep," and "black day," what is he likely to learn about the evaluative aspect of "blackness"? Clearly, the child whose linguistic environment is different will learn a different reaction to "blackness."

Let's look at the origin of just one such disposition gained by classical conditioning and demonstrate how this disposition is aroused in cue control NSI. Before we do that, however, a brief review of the classical conditioning process is in order. Of course, the most common illustration of classical conditioning is the case of Pavlov's hound (1927). Pavlov trained a dog to salivate (a desirable goal, I guess) at the sound of a bell by pairing the sound of the bell with the presentation of meat powder over a number of trials. Initially, the meat powder was necessary for the dog to salivate, but after a number of associations of bell and meat powder, the bell was sufficient to elicit the response. In other words, the dog's response, salivation, was transferred or generalized from the powder to the bell. Thus, the result of classical conditioning is the transfer of cues capable of eliciting a specific response.

That dogs are not the only animals susceptible to this kind of learning was illustrated by Staats and Staats (1958). They paired positive words (beauty, gift, happy, and health) and negative words (sour, agony, disgusting, and dirty) with national names, such as Dutch, German, and British. As expected, after a number of trials the national names associated with negative words came to be evaluated negatively, and those national names associated with positive words were soon viewed as positive. In sum, Staats and Staats established a disposition within the subjects on the basis of their particular experience. They learned a disposition: certain national names are positive and certain others are negative. Assume for a moment that the subjects were conditioned to be positively disposed to the national name "British" and negatively disposed to the national name "German." Further assume that you were a travel agent and met those subjects as they left the experiment. Do you think you would be more successful in convincing these subjects to travel to Britain or Germany? Obviously, such a decision is a complex one and would involve many factors, such as how much money the trips cost. But the cues in your message (the national names) would probably elicit a disposition or tendency in favor of travel in Britain and in opposition to travel in Germany.

Many dispositions of thought and action are established through the learning experiences of an individual, and these dispositions can be "called out" or made salient in the cue control process. The relationship of learning theories and attitude formation and change has been extensively discussed elsewhere, and the predictions based on this model have, in general, been well supported (Weiss, 1968).

Expectations. Take the following Test of Everyday Expectations. For each question select the letter of the most probable answer.

1. If you saw an old lady kicking a dog, she
   a) is defending herself from the dog's attack
   b) is attacking the dog

2. A likes B, B likes C, so
   a) A likes C
   b) A does not like C
3. George just bought a Chevrolet. Therefore,
   a) George preferred the Chevrolet to the equally priced Ford
   b) George preferred the equally priced Ford to the Chevrolet
4. Both Harold and Pete belong to the same fraternity, have the same major, play football, and belong to the Young Democrats Alliance. Therefore,
   a) they like each other
   b) they dislike each other
5. The next number in the series 2, 4, 8, 16, —— is
   a) 32
   b) 48
   c) 3.5
6. Clarence ran nude through downtown Bigotsville as part of his fraternity's "Hell Week" to become a full-fledged member:
   a) Clarence wanted to become a fraternity member.
   b) Clarence did not want to become a fraternity member.
7. Sue is living with Sam:
   a) Sue likes Sam
   b) Sue does not like Sam.

Because of extensive experience with many situations that have common attributes, people derive expectations of what "goes with" what or what means what. For instance, most people pick "a" as the answer to all of the questions on the preceding test. Look back and see if you can identify the generalization or expectations that account for such uniformity of response. The expectations that account for the answer "a" in each case might be something like these:

1. Old ladies don't attack dogs.
2. Mutual friends usually like each other.
3. People don't buy things they don't want.
4. Similar people usually like each other.
5. The future is based on the past.
6. People don't work for things they don't want.
7. People live with people they like.

Obviously, you have many such expectations or associations that you have learned over time. An influencer can rely on the existence of these expectations and exercise influence by providing the cues which make these expectations salient. For example, Schein *et al.* (1961) noted the role of expectations in the "brainwashing" attempts of the Chinese Communists in North Korea. People do not expect nations they love and fight for to do certain types of evil things, nor do they expect enemy countries to do certain types of good things. A violation of these expectations produces a good deal of psychological confusion and increases one's susceptibility to influence. Shein *et al.* (1961) observed that "this technique was clearly seen in the POW camps where all publications, news broadcasts, movies, mail, and contact with outsiders was carefully filtered for its ideological purity. Western literature and personal mail were permitted only if they supported the communist ideology or could serve some other important function, e.g. mail was permitted to go through which contained bad news in order to demoralize the prisoner and to undermine the support which he might be getting from identification with reference groups."* Information which showed democracy as decadent and immoral and communism as moral and desirable (a violation of expectations for U.S. troops) was not only allowed, but was used as a cue to elicit anti-American and pro-Communist feelings. But cue control relying on expectations is not limited to brainwashing.

Advertising researchers have obviously concluded that people expect things that smell like lemons to be clean and

---

*Schein, *et al.*, *Coercive Persuasion*, p. 80. Reprinted by permission.

fresh, as evidenced by the fact that everything from car wax to calendars is associated with lemons in recent commercials. As reported earlier, a similar expectation is made of detergent that comes in blue-and-yellow boxes. Expectations of self and others are a powerful force not only in the interpretation of social situations, response to influence attempts, and the formation of impressions of other people, but also on perception itself. Bruner and Postman (1966) presented a number of pictures on a screen with a tachistoscope (a device that permits a researcher to present a visual image for a predetermined duration of time, e.g., 10 milliseconds, 30 milliseconds, etc.). The images were of playing cards. One set of images was of perfectly normal cards. The other set of pictures reversed the normal color of the cards, e.g., a black five-of-hearts, a red six-of-clubs, etc. The researchers wanted to discover whether it took longer to recognize the incongruous cards than the congruous cards. Indeed, the average presentation speed at recognition for the congruous cards (28 milliseconds) was much shorter than for the incongruous ones (114 milliseconds). Bruner and Postman concluded that their research provided "a reaffirmation of the general statement that perceptual organization is powerfully determined by expectations built upon past commerce with the environment" (1966, p. 291). If a person wants to influence another, he may determine the expectations of that person and provide the cues that make the desired response probable.

Attitudes. "Attitude" has been defined in a variety of ways over the years of its prominence as an important psychological construct. However, if you examine the following three definitions of "attitude," you will note an important similarity; each characterizes "attitude" as a disposition.

- *"An attitude is a mental and neural state of readiness, organized through experience, exerting a directive or dynamic influence upon the individual's response to all objects and situations with which it is related"* (Allport, 1967, p. 8).

- "Attitude is an implicit response with drive strength which occurs within the individual as a reaction to stimulus patterns and which affects subsequent overt responses" (Doob, 1967, p. 43).

- "Attitudes are learned predispositions to respond to an object or class of objects in a favorable or unfavorable way" (Fishbein, 1967, p. 257).

Regardless of the definition preferred, an attitude is a *disposition;* it tends to direct reaction to a situation or object one way or another. Therefore, when attitudes are made salient, they bias action and thought. Aronson and Golden (1962), for example, found that for prejudiced subjects (who presumably had negative dispositions or attitudes toward blacks), a black person was less influential than was a white person in a typical social-influence situation. This result is even more startling when it is discovered that the four sources employed in this experiment were (1) a white engineer, (2) a black engineer, (3) a white dishwasher, and (4) a black dishwasher and that the topic of the speech was "arithmetic." The prejudiced subjects were more influenced by the white dishwasher than by the black engineer.

Thought and action are strongly affected by the disposition called "attitude." Again, knowledge is power in cue control, and knowledge of another's attitudes provides one with great power. The arousal of specific attitudes by providing appropriate cues designed to make certain attitudes salient is one of the most well-researched phenomena and will receive more complete treatment later in this chapter.

Dispositions: A Reconsideration

Let's re-examine some of the examples in the preceding discussion of dispositions.

Disposition: Cultural norm; Siblings protect and support each other.
　　Observed behavior: You disliked Clyde for calling your sister a "hooker."

Disposition: Well-learned response; "German" is an undesirable characteristic.

Observed behavior: Subjects preferred to travel to Britain than to Germany.

Disposition: Expectation; Things that smell "lemony" are fresh and clean.

Observed behavior: People buy products that smell lemony.

Disposition: Attitude; Prejudiced subjects are negatively disposed toward blacks.

Observed behavior: Prejudiced subjects were more persuaded by a white source than by a black source.

In these situations the observed behavior appears consistent with the disposition. It would be inconsistent, would it not, for you to like Clyde for calling your sister a "hooker"; for subjects to travel to the less preferred country; for people to buy something other than that which they expect to be clean and fresh; or for prejudiced subjects to be more persuaded by a black source than a white one? All of the reactions, given the dispositions held, appear natural and "make sense." All of the preceding discussion illustrates the underlying principle of cognitive consistency. The drive for cognitive consistency is the overriding disposition.

The Principle of Cognitive Consistency: The Overriding Disposition

The theoretical position to be discussed in this section is an integration of the basic principles common to a large number of similar theories. Beginning in the 1940s and continuing to the present, theory and research in many areas of concern have produced many theories with the common underlying notion that people tend to organize cognitive elements (attitudes, beliefs, values, and behavior) into a relatively consistent system. Additionally, these theories have all posited that people try to maintain this state of internal consistency and avoid the condition of cognitive inconsistency. These basic propositions are common to the theories of balance (Heider, 1946, 1958), symmetry (Newcomb, 1953, 1956), congruity (Osgood and Tannenbaum, 1955), and cognitive dissonance (Festinger, 1957), to name those most important.* This section will present a synthesis of these theories, with an admittedly greater reliance on the theory of cognitive dissonance.

Two distinctive features of human cognitive organization are its *connectedness* and its *coherence* (Aronson, 1972). The characterization of connectedness is derived from the everyday observation that everyone seems, in varying degrees, to be predictable; if you know just a few things about a person, such as his political party preference, income, age, sex, and occupation, you can occasionally predict a wide variety of other characteristics. For instance, is a young, single woman who is well educated, a Democrat, and a strong supporter of the Equal Rights Amendment more likely to oppose or favor liberalized abortion laws? People are predictable because within their cognitive structure, there seems to be some coherent or understandable organizational scheme. The most obvious organizational scheme or pattern of coherence appears to be that of cognitive consistency—people try to be internally consistent.

Cognitive consistency (called "balance," "symmetry," "congruence," or "consonance" by other theorists) is a state achieved when connected or related cognitions "fit together" or when one cognition implies or follows from another. For example, the cognition that I do not like eggplant is consistent with the fact that I do not eat eggplant. The cognition that George did not vote for the antipollution initiative, which I strongly supported, is consistent with the fact that I do not like George. Conversely, cognitive inconsistency ("imbalance," "asymmetry," "incongruence," or "dissonance") occurs whenever two connected cognitions do not "fit together," such as knowing that you do not like the color red, but buying a red car or finding out that your best friend has been spreading malicious stories about you. When one cognition does not follow from or is not implied by another, cognitive inconsistency is felt by an individual. Of course, the rule of coherence or consis-

---

*For a full treatment of cognitive consistency theories, see Abelson *et al.* (1968), and Insko (1967).

tency does not apply when cognitions are not connected or perceived to relate to one another. Your view on the Mid-East conflict, for instance, is probably unrelated to your preference for a particular flavor of milkshake. Thus, cognitive consistency occurs when cognitions are connected *and* coherent, whereas cognitive inconsistency occurs when cognitions are connected but not coherent.

A note of caution must be raised at this juncture in the explanation. Though there has been much debate on this question, it appears that the most useful conception of inconsistency is psychological, not strictly logical. That is, many circumstances produce a felt inconsistency that are not logically inconsistent according to the rules of formal logic. As mentioned throughout this book, people's perception of "reality," rather than the objective "reality," governs behavior. In this case, what *appears* "logical" or "illogical" is more important than whether it actually is logical or illogical. Aronson (1968) demonstrated this point well with an illustration. If you learned that your favorite novelist beat his wife, would that create an internal inconsistency for you? For some, this knowledge may create a felt inconsistency because their conception of a "great novelist" evokes an image of a compassionate, sensitive person, and wife-beating is neither. For others, however, the writer's private behavior is irrelevant or unrelated to his products, great novels, on which their opinion rests. Thus, although your evaluation of writing quality and your knowledge that your favorite author beats his wife are not *logically* related, these two cognitions may or may not produce psychological inconsistency. Another way to conceive of psychological inconsistency is to argue that a violation of expectation produces inconsistency. In sum, the basic issue is this: Can two cognitions be maintained simultaneously? If not, cognitive inconsistency occurs. If so, no cognitive inconsistency occurs. This rather imprecise definition of the crucial state of cognitive inconsistency has been both the basis for much of the criticism of cognitive consistency theories and the reason the theory has been applicable in so many behavioral domains. Nevertheless, consistency is a state of coherent (understandable) connectedness between cognitions, and inconsistency is a state which occurs when cognitions are connected but not coherent. So what? Do these states mean anything to the individual experiencing them?

The power of cognitive consistency theories lies in their explanation of the effects of the states of inconsistency and consistency, not in the definition of those states. The effect or psychological importance of inconsistency is captured by the following propositions:

1. Inconsistency is a psychologically uncomfortable state and produces a drive to reduce inconsistency and restore a condition of cognitive coherence or consistency.

2. The strength of the drive to reduce inconsistency is a function of the degree of importance attached to the inconsistent elements and the number of cognitive elements affected by the inconsistency.

The importance and power of these relatively simple propositions concerning the effects of inconsistency is evidenced by the amount of research they have generated.* Before you assume, however, that inconsistency reduction is the single dominant force motivating human behavior and the key to understanding all instances of social influence, as some have done, you should recognize a few limitations to these propositions. As with all other partial explanations of human behavior, this drive to reduce inconsistency is not absolute, nor does inconsistency always demand reduction.

First, there appear to be some circumstances in which people seek the state of inconsistency (Bem, 1970; Berlyne, 1960; Fowler, 1965). That is, novelty and inconsistency are often actually sought out—"consistency is the hobgoblin of little minds." The specific psychological and situational determinants of inconsistency-seeking are not fully understood yet, and any generalization concerning these effects at this time would be dubious. Second, if the importance of the inconsistent elements is not great, no effort will be expended to relieve it. If you

---

*Many bibliographies of research concerning the effects of cognitive consistency have been compiled. The bibliography in *Theories of Cognitive Consistency: A Sourcebook*, (Abelson, *et al.*, 1968), for instance, has over 1000 entries.

discovered that you and your friend differed in the evaluation of the relative merits of red and yellow jello, obviously your life would not be catastrophically upset. On the other hand, in the unlikely situation that you and your friend disagreed about the war in Indochina or the importance of pollution control, you might be compelled to reduce the inconsistency in some manner. Third, there is even a problem or limitation that has a name —the discrepancy problem. Specifically, the prediction of behavior from knowledge of attitudes is often inaccurate; people don't "practice what they preach." The discrepancy between attitudes and behavior could pose a serious challenge to cognitive consistency theories, except for two developments: (1) promising theoretic and methodological advancements (Fishbein, 1973; Ajzen and Fishbein, 1973), and (2) the recognition that no single theory, especially one as simple as the cognitive consistency theory, can account for all behavior at all times of all people. Finally, as this book has tried to emphasize, there are *many* forces operating on an individual, and inconsistency reduction is just one of those forces. Frequently, other, contradictory forces are more demanding than the need to restore consistency, and these other forces direct behavior. Or, even more frequently, numerous forces operate simultaneously, and manifest behavior is the result of not just one but many factors. Hobgoblin or not, however, inconsistency reduction is an important force in human behavior, especially in response to social influence attempts.

Given that inconsistency is psychologically uncomfortable and produces a drive to restore consistency, it is logical that people would actively avoid situations that would increase inconsistency and would actively seek situations that tend to reduce inconsistency. A number of researchers have demonstrated the validity of these implications, but one of the most obvious was a study by Ehrlich, Guttman, Schonback, and Mills (1957). They observed the behavior of people who had just bought a new car and found that the buyers selectively exposed themselves to ads of the car they had just purchased and avoided the ads for cars they had to reject in their final decision. Consider the position of the person who just decided to buy a Chevrolet rather than a Ford. The cars were of comparable styling and engineering, had similar features, and were about the same price. He decided to buy the Chevrolet, which included the lighted ashtray that was unavailable in the Ford, but he did not get the lockable spare tire holder in the Chevrolet that the Ford featured. "Oh well," he said like the fox in Aesop's fable, "I don't get many flat tires anyway." The next morning while reading the newspaper, he saw a Chevrolet ad, read it, agreed with it, and felt good about his decision. On the next page, there was a Ford ad. Is reading that ad going to make him feel good about having bought a Chevrolet? Hell no! So he skipped it. When he got to work, would you predict he had lunch with a person who had just bought a new Ford or one who had just bought a new Chevrolet?

The next obvious question, is "O.K., so people don't like inconsistency but do like consistency and seek it. What specific things do people do when their cognitive state is inconsistent?" The modes of inconsistency reduction have been the topic of much research attention and theoretic debate, and the issue has yet to be settled. But several modes of inconsistency reduction are well documented and bear importantly on the operation of social influence. To illustrate these different modes of inconsistency reduction, a hypothetical situation will be set up.

I happen to like to eat fish, all kinds of fish (except catfish). Whether it is from the ocean, a lake, a stream, or even a hatchery pond, I like fish. The other day a Dr. Theodore Testtube, a very trustworthy and competent researcher for the Food and Drug Administration, announced that the consumption of any fish was tantamount to suicide because of the high level of pollutants fish now contain. He said that mercury, DDT, and various other pesticides and herbicides have all been found at significant levels in the tested fish and that eating these fish is a very real health hazard. If you could have looked into my head at the conclusion of hearing the announcement, you might have seen the following:

Cognition 1: I like to eat fish.
Cognition 2: Fish is unhealthful to eat.

Obviously, I felt a good deal of inconsistency (given that I am not stupid, I should not do things contrary to my own health). Consequently, I had to do something to restore consistency. Here are a few of the things I might do:

1. I could *change my behavior.* * I could quit eating fish. By so doing, the internal picture would look like this:

    Cognition 1: I do not eat fish.
    Cognition 2: Fish is unhealthful to eat.

This is perfectly consistent. By changing my behavior I have restored coherence or consistency and have reduced the anxiety associated with inconsistency.

2. I could *change my evaluation of the source.* I could conclude that Dr. Testtube is an incompetent researcher and that he does not know what he is talking about. Having rejected Dr. Testtube, and thereby his report, I can still believe that fish is perfectly healthful, which would be consistent with my behavior, eating fish.

These are the easy resolutions of inconsistency. There are also a few complex ways to reduce or make less important the felt inconsistency.

3. I could *deny, repress, or reject the proposition* that eating fish is unhealthful. I can still maintain my faith in Dr. Testtube, but merely reject the statement of fact. Admittedly, this is a difficult trick of mental gymnastics and is increasingly difficult as the objective reality or obviousness of the fact increases, such as seeing a friend get ill from eating fish, but it is still a possibility. I could also deny that I ever liked fish. In this case, I would not change from positive to negative, just deny I ever liked it.

4. I could *differentiate.* That is, I could divide the object of controversy into two or more discernable units. For example, I could conclude that Dr. Testtube was talking about ocean fish and I could continue to eat fresh-water fish, or I could decide that he was talking about Atlantic Ocean fish and not Pacific Ocean fish.

---

* If an attitude rather than a behavior were involved in the inconsistent relationship, the mode of inconsistency reduction would be a *change in attitude.*

5. I could *bolster.* I could support, or bolster, my behavior by attaching it to another cognition and attribute greater importance to the newly relevant cognition. For example, I might conclude that maybe eating fish is a little unhealthful but that it is very good and it is very cheap when compared to other main dishes. Thus, the continuation of my behavior, eating fish, is related to other things such as saving money or a preference for good-tasting things. This tactic does not get rid of the inconsistency; it just submerges it in a larger consistency.

6. I could *transcend.* That is, I could relieve the pressure of the inconsistency by relying on a higher principle such as saying to myself, "That is silly; when my time comes, it comes, and what I eat will make little difference."

7. I could *stop thinking about it.* I could simply put the inconsistency out of mind and continue as I always have.

8. I could *live with it and make a virtue out of it.* For example, I could, as have so many smokers, admit I am doing something dangerous but in so doing appear daring, dashing, brave, and masculine (only brave men do potentially dangerous things on purpose). (Another example of the Audie Murphy syndrome?)

One of the tasks of the remainder of this chapter will be an attempt to discover what determines the specific mode of resolution chosen in given circumstances.

Cue Control Revisited

Within each individual there exist many dispositions, and those dispositions are organized according to an overriding disposition toward cognitive consistency. Cue control NSI is a manipulative form of social influence in which the influencer provides cues that make certain of the target's dispositions salient in the direction of behavior. "Opportunities to exercise cue control," according to Jones and Gerard (1967), "arise out of the recipient's past history of commerce with outcomes in the presence of cues that the controller is now able to provide" (p. 532). Cue control influence, whether in situations of persuasion, advertising, interpersonal bargaining, or whatever, appears to have three crucial dimensions:

1. The believability of the suggested assertion.
2. The magnitude of inconsistency produced.
3. The mode of resolution chosen.

For example, both temporally and conceptually, in the "fish story" presented earlier, the first question is "Do I or do I not believe the assertion that the consumption of fish is unhealthful?" If I believe it, the next question is the degree, or magnitude, or inconsistency produced by the connection of the two inconsistent cognitions. Finally, given that the magnitude of felt inconsistency is sufficient to demand resolution, which mode of resolution will be chosen, and what limitation of my choice is imposed by the influencer? The psychological, sociological, situational, cultural, and biological factors that relate to these questions concerning cue control NSI will be the focus of the remainder of this chapter.

PSYCHOLOGICAL FACTORS

Acceptance

The relationship between the psychological characteristics of the target and his acceptance of a suggested premise (e.g., "Fish are unhealthful to eat.") is not well understood. However, a few tentative generalizations are suggested by the research.

First, and most obviously, people are more likely to accept an advocated premise if it is consistent with their present cognitive structure. That is, people will accept those things that will not produce inconsistency. Feather (1964), for example, found that people accepted or rejected arguments on the basis of the consistency principle. If an argument supported their position, they accepted it; if it did not support their position, they rejected it. In short, people accept more readily those premises or arguments that will not necessitate cognitive work.

Second, Siegel, Miller, and Wotring (1969) suggested that receivers differ in their sensitivity to the differences among high- and low-credible sources or influencers. Some people appear to be *credibility prone;* they are particularly susceptible to influence from high-credible sources and unusually resistant to influence from low-credible sources. People low in this characteristic, those not credibility prone, are not as sensitive to the differences among influencers and are, correspondingly, less affected by the credibility of the source and more reliant on the message itself. Credibility-prone individuals are more likely to accept an advocated proposition from a high-credible source than is a person low on the credibility-prone dimension. The same type of relationship is suggested by the research for the variables of authoritarianism and dogmatism.

When the influencer is perceived as an "authority," high-authoritarian and the high-dogmatic persons are more likely to accept the advocated proposition than are low-authoritarians and low-dogmatics. Conversely, when the influencer is not perceived as an "authority," high-authoritarians and high-dogmatics are less likely to accept a premise than are those low on either characteristic. In sum, a person with high credibility proneness, high authoritarianism, or high dogmatism attends a great deal to "who said it" and not as much to "what was said" and is more likely to accept an advocated proposition if the source is perceived as an "authority." People low on these three characteristics typically respond on the basis of message content rather than the origin of the message and do not, therefore, accept arguments merely because they came from a particular source.

Magnitude of Inconsistency

A person's tolerance for inconsistency is a crucial variable in the cognitive consistency paradigm of human behavior. Remember, the greater the perceived magnitude of inconsistency, the greater the probability of change. To the extent that a person has a high tolerance for inconsistency, the less the perceived magnitude of the inconsistency and the less he feels pressure to deal with manifest inconsistency. Imagine, for instance, two people who just discovered that their best friend had been telling everybody that they were not very bright. Some inconsistency must exist in their cognitive structure. If one person had a high tolerance for inconsistency, he might just shrug off the inconsistency and not be affected by it. If the other individual had a low tolerance for inconsistency, he might feel compelled to reduce the inconsistency by some means, e.g., misperceive the reported comments, change his attitude toward his friend, argue with his friend, etc. Indeed, the individual differences in tolerance for inconsistency is an important aspect in determining response to inconsistency. Five psychological variables probably affect an individual's tolerance for inconsistency—authoritarianism, dogmatism, anxiety, self-esteem, and ego-involvement. Authoritarianism and dogmatism can be discussed together.

Authoritarian and dogmatic people tend to engage in simple "black-and-white" thinking. It is reasonable to assume, therefore, that an inconsistency, which can be maintained only by relatively complex mental gymnastics, would be more difficult for high-authoritarians and high-dogmatics to live with than for people low in either characteristic. Indeed, research supports this conclusion (Foulkes and Foulkes, 1965; Steiner and Johnson, 1963). Miller and Rokeach (1968) probably summarized the relationship best when they concluded that "authoritarian and dogmatic persons should thus seek to structure situations in cognitively consistent and simple ways. Furthermore, inconsistent stimuli should be rejected, distorted, ignored, or denied. By contrast, equalitarian and low dogmatic individuals should be able to tolerate more cognitive inconsistency because of their greater ability to think complexly and in an integrated fashion" (p. 625).

On the assumption that decreased tolerance for inconsistency results in increased susceptibility to influence, the research in persuasion supports the indicated relationship between authoritarianism and dogmatism and tolerance for inconsistency. When the source of influence is regarded as an "authority," high-authoritarians and dogmatics are more susceptible to influence than are lows on both of these personality characteristics. But when the source of influence is not regarded as an "authority," inconsistency is presumably not induced in high-authoritarians and high-dogmatics, and they have been shown to be less influenced than low-authoritarians and low-dogmatics. Put simply, high-authoritarians and high-dogmatics have a low tolerance for inconsistency and are, therefore, more susceptible to influence.

On an intuitive basis there appears to be little difference between the psychological state of inconsistency and the psychological state of anxiety. Logically, tolerance for inconsistency should be related to (1) the tolerance for anxiety, and (2) the amount of base anxiety upon which situational inconsistency is added. The first point, the relationship between tolerance for inconsistency and tolerance for anxiety, is not well understood and relates to one's entire adaptation to life and stress, which is beyond the scope of this book. The second point, however, is clearly related to social influence, and answers are available. The research shows that persons high in normal anxiety are more susceptible to influence than are nonanxious persons. Apparently, the inconsistency induced by a particular influence situation is of greater magnitude when the person is already anxious than if he is not anxious. When an inconsistency is added to already extant anxiety, it creates an inconsistency more demanding of resolution than if the person were not anxious to begin with. In short, pre-existing anxiety reduces a person's tolerance for inconsistency and increases the probability of influence.

Another determinant of the tolerance for inconsistency is self-esteem. Research has found a relationship between low self-esteem and the probability of influence. Specifically, the individual with high self-esteem is less susceptible to influence than the person with low self-esteem.* Individuals with high self-esteem can tolerate inconsistency because they feel self-confident that they could handle it if they were forced to deal with it at some later time, such as when they talk to someone about it (Rosen and Wyer, 1972). Persons with low self-esteem are not confident in their ability to live with an inconsistency

---

*Some of the research suggests an inverted-U relationship between self-esteem and influence (Triandis, 1971, p. 176). The differences in results appear to be a function of a "ceiling effect": how high does self-esteem have to be before it is "high self-esteem?" This should be an area of considerable future research.

successfully, and they therefore work to reduce it. Persons with high self-esteem have a higher tolerance for inconsistency than do persons with low self-esteem.

The "self " affects one's tolerance for inconsistency in yet another manner. Everyone has cognitions about themselves (we do good things, we make wise decisions, we are good lovers, etc.), and inconsistencies involving these cognitions produce a greater perceived magnitude of inconsistency than do those inconsistencies not involving self-oriented cognitions. Bramel (1968) noted that "most dissonance experiments have induced the subjects to behave in ways that lead both to disconfirmation of expectation about oneself and to the arousal of implications that one's behavior has been incompetent or immoral" (p. 365). Thus, the motive to save face maximizes the perceived magnitude of an inconsistency involving self-oriented cognitions. A person's tolerance for consistency is lower when "self" is involved in the inconsistency.

Finally, the variable of ego-involvement is related to the tolerance for inconsistency. As mentioned earlier, the magnitude of the drive to reduce inconsistency is, in part, a function of the importance of the cognitive elements involved. Ego-involvement is a measure of the importance an individual attaches to a given cognition. The research demonstrates that individuals with low ego-involvement are more susceptible to influence than are highly ego-involved persons (Rhine and Severence, 1970; Sereno, 1968). This seems to be a contradiction at first glance, for if highly ego-involved persons have a low tolerance for inconsistency, then they should be more susceptible to influence. The resolution to this problem was suggested by Sereno (1968). The highly ego-involved person is very resistant to changing the attitude in which he is highly ego-involved; thus he appears less susceptible to influence. But he is more likely to change his evaluation of the source of the discrepant communication than is the person with low ego-involvement. That is, the highly ego-involved person experiences inconsistency, has a low tolerance for inconsistency, and is reluctant to change the cognition in which he is involved; therefore, he derogates the source. Highly ego-involved persons have a low tolerance for inconsistency that deals with the highly involving cognitions, but manifest this low tolerance in ways other than changing their attitudes.

In conclusion, if we wanted to build a person with the highest possible tolerance for inconsistency, he would be a non-anxious individual who is neither authoritarian nor dogmatic, is not ego-involved, and has a high level of self-esteem. Even if this person accepted the premise of an argument and some inconsistency was induced, he would laugh at the inconsistency and walk away unaffected by the experience.

Resolution of Inconsistency

When a person accepts the argument of an influencer and the resultant inconsistency is of sufficient magnitude to require resolution, the individual has many potential modes of inconsistency reduction. The influencer will be more effective to the extent that one particular mode of resolution, the desired goal, is chosen over all the other possible means of inconsistency reduction. For example, earlier Dr. Testtube desired that people quit eating fish and presented a message with that goal in mind. But even if a person accepted that fish are unhealthful to eat and felt an inconsistency that demanded resolution, he would have many options besides changing his behavior. He could reject Dr. Testtube as a credible source, bolster, etc. Little is known of a generalized preference for a particular mode of inconsistency reduction, but it is assumed to exist, as people have typical response tendencies to so many other situations. There are, however, three general "rules" that seem apparent.

First, when a person experiences inconsistency, he will generally choose the resolution mode that involves the least psychological effort. Again, if you and your friend differed in your evaluation of the relative merits of two flavors of ice cream and it was sufficiently upsetting so as to demand some form of resolution, which would be more likely: changing your attitude about a particular flavor of ice cream, or changing your attitude toward your friend? Obviously, changing your attitude toward the ice cream is less psychologically demanding and difficult than changing your attitude toward your friend. Is it easier to reject the Surgeon General as a valid source of information, or to quit smoking? Most people have chosen the resolution mode that involves the least effort and have derogated the Surgeon General rather than quit smoking.

One measure of the effort required in changing thought or action is the relative importance of a particular cognition, or level of ego-involvement. Ego-involvement is the degree of importance a particular cognition plays in one's cognitive structure. Research has consistently shown that highly ego-involved subjects are less persuadable on the topic of their involvement than are subjects with low ego-involvement. Thus, one translation of the proposition that people prefer the least effort mode of resolution is to argue that the mode of resolution affecting the cognition of lowest ego-involvement will be preferred.

Second, a slightly different type of the least-effort principle also appears to affect the selection of a particular mode of resolution. *People choose the resolution mode that will require the least effort to maintain in the long run.* People apparently anticipate the difficulty of maintaining consistency via a particular mode of inconsistency reduction and select that mode which entails the least effort in the future. In the example of Dr. Testtube's fishy warning, since one can easily anticipate the difficulty involved in rejecting the data or denying Dr. Testtube's credibility, especially if people get sick from eating fish, that method of resolution might not be the best. The more difficult it will be to maintain a particular mode of resolution, the less likely it is that that mode will be chosen.

Finally, Burnstein (1967) has suggested that *people have a "positivity bias" in the selection mode of inconsistency reduction.* By this, he means that attitudes are more often changed from negative to positive than in the opposite direction. If you disliked Clyde and your friend liked him, it is more likely that you would change your evaluation of Clyde from negative to positive than change your evaluation of your friend from positive to negative. This is a tentative conclusion, but it is consistent with other psychological data (e.g., the cultural bias toward accommodation in interpersonal conflicts).

What mode of inconsistency reduction will be chosen in any given situation? The answer is still incomplete, but *probably* the selection will favor the mode that involves the least effort, both immediately and in the long run, and that results in changes from negative to positive.

SOCIOLOGICAL FACTORS

In this section we will explore the antecedents and consequences of only one variable, *source credibility*. Admittedly, the perceived status or similarity of the influencer will affect the probability of influence, but the greatest bulk of research and theory concerning the influencer-target relationship in cue control has focused on the attribution of source credibility.

Source credibility is a set of perceptions held by the target person about an influencer. Source credibility is not something possessed by an influencer, but is another person's view, or image, of an influencer. It is evident, therefore, that for any given source, individuals may differ in their perception of his credibility. For example, within any public gathering listening to any political candidate, there will be those listeners who regard the speaker as credible and those who perceive the speaker as not credible. Think of a group that would probably regard Richard Nixon as credible, if you can. Is that group likely to regard any of the Chicago Seven as credible?

Source credibility is not a single-dimension perception. Rather, it is a composite perception involving three relatively independent factors. The most consistent estimate to date is that source credibility is composed of perceptions of *competence, trustworthiness,* and *dynamism.* * The competence factor accounts for the perception of another's intelligence and knowledge. This factor is probably the reason that source credibility is topic-specific; that is, a particular source may be perceived as competent on topic A, but not on topic B, whereas another source may be perceived as competent on topic B, but not on topic A. Dr. Benjamin Spock, for instance, might be

---

*The discovery and specification of the dimensions of source credibility is an area of extensive current investigation. The actual dimensions of source credibility are probably different for different types of sources. See J. C. McCroskey, T. Jensen, and C. Valencia, "Measurement of the Credibility of Peers and Spouses," a paper presented at the International Communication Association Convention, Montreal, 1973; J. C. McCroskey and T. Jensen, "Measurement of the Credibility of Mass Media Sources," a paper presented at the Western Speech Communication Association Convention, Albuquerque, 1973.

viewed by some as competent on the topic of child-rearing practices, but few would regard him as an expert on the topic of world economics. The trustworthiness factor of source credibility refers to the perception of the source's character, friendliness, and fairness. The third, and probably least important factor of source credibility, dynamism, refers to the perception of the source's energy, boldness, and confidence. Figure 4–1 contains examples of the scales used to measure the perceived competence, trustworthiness, and dynamism of a source.

INDIVIDUAL SOURCE

Competence:

intelligent	—	—	—	—	—	—	—	unintelligent
informed	—	—	—	—	—	—	—	uninformed
qualified	—	—	—	—	—	—	—	unqualified

Trustworthiness:

just	—	—	—	—	—	—	—	unjust
fair	—	—	—	—	—	—	—	unfair
ethical	—	—	—	—	—	—	—	unethical

Dynamism:

energetic	—	—	—	—	—	—	—	tired
active	—	—	—	—	—	—	—	passive
bold	—	—	—	—	—	—	—	timid

Fig. 4–1 Representative scales for the measurement of source credibility.

To summarize, the source credibility attributed to an individual is an extremely important factor in social influence by means of cue control. Source credibility is a set of perceptions about an influencer and not a possession of the influencer. It is topic-specific and is based on the factors of competence, trustworthiness, and dynamism. The importance of source credibility in the operation of cue control NSI can be illustrated in two ways.

First, let's adapt the basic structural balance model (one of the cognitive consistency models) to show how important source credibility is. If you liked Clyde and both you and Clyde liked anthropology, the situation could be diagramed as follows:

ANTHROPOLOGY

\+   \+

You   \+   Clyde

Heider (1946), the originator of such an analysis, contended that this situation would be cognitively consistent, or balanced, in that it involved three positive attitudes or relations. According to Heider, all situations involving either three positive relations or two negative relations and one positive relation are cognitively consistent. All other relations are cognitively inconsistent. Using this analytic scheme, let's examine the effects of source credibility. Given that you think Clyde is credible (You+Clyde), what happens when Clyde contends either that he likes or dislikes economics as a major? (See Fig. 4–2.)

ECONOMICS   ECONOMICS

\+   –

You   \+   Clyde   You   \+   Clyde

Figure 4–2

If you behave so as to maintain cognitive consistency, as Heider defined it, what would your reactions to both situations be? Wouldn't you agree with Clyde in both cases? (See Fig. 4–3).

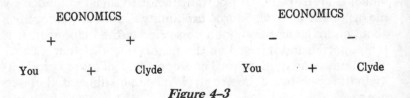

ECONOMICS   ECONOMICS

\+   \+   –   –

You   \+   Clyde   You   \+   Clyde

Figure 4–3

Similarly, if you did not think Clyde was a credible source (You – Clyde), your attempts to maintain balance would result in inevitable disagreement with Clyde (see Fig. 4–4).

ECONOMICS   ECONOMICS

+   –   –   +

You   –   Clyde   You   –   Clyde

Figure 4–4

Clearly, this analysis suggests that the credibility of a given source is a strong predisposing factor toward either agreement or disagreement with a source. Indeed, testimonial advertising has relied for years on this simple process. When a famous athlete says on television that he likes a new chocolate bar, the advertisers are hoping that the audience's initial attraction to the athlete will cause such machinations to take place in the heads of the receivers.

Another way to demonstrate the importance of source credibility is to go back to the three crucial dimensions of social influence identified earlier in this chapter—the acceptance of the suggested premise, the magnitude of inconsistency produced, and the mode of inconsistency resolution selected. Simply, the acceptance of an argument or premise is more likely with high-credible sources than with low-credible sources; the magnitude of inconsistency is likely to be greater with a credible source than with a low-credible source; and the more credible the source of influence, the less likely the derogation of the source as a mode of inconsistency resolution. Rather than discuss the general import of source credibility, let's examine the specific impact of source credibility.

Of course, the major effect of source credibility is that the greater the perceived source credibility of an influencer, the greater the probability and/or amount of influence. High-credible sources induce greater influence than do low-credible sources. However, the effects of source credibility on influence are apparently very short-term (Hovland and Weiss, 1951; Kel-

man and Hovland, 1953). That is, the effects of credibility diminish over time (see Fig. 4–5).

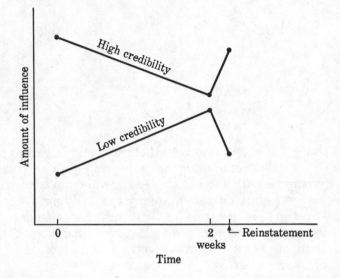

Fig. 4–5 The sleeper effect and source-message reinstatement.

This reduction of impact is known as the "sleeper effect";
over time, people disassociate the source of a message and the
content of the message. The immediate improvement provided
by high credibility and the immediate decrement associated
with low credibility become less important as people forget the
connection between message content and a particular source.
The effects of credibility can be restored by reminding people
where they heard the argument (see Fig. 4–5). Your own experiences probably confirm the "sleeper effect." Have you ever
forgotten where or from whom you heard something, only to
either believe it more or reject it as foolish when you remembered from whom you heard it? Most people have and do. One
crucial question remains: Why is one perceived as either highly
or negligibly credible?

There are two identifiable origins of the perception of
source credibility: the view an audience has of a source prior to

the influence attempt, and the view generated during the influence attempt. The former is based on *extrinsic factors of source credibility;* the latter is based on *factors intrinsic to the influence situation.*

Extrinsic factors of source credibility are numerous. An individual may hold a particular view of another person because of prior experience with that person, a title he holds, the groups he belongs to, and, even, the credibility of the person who introduces him. Extrinsic factors of source credibility are important in at least two ways. First, it is on the basis of this extrinsic source credibility that a person will either expose himself or avoid the influence situation. For example, if you heard that someone you thought of as stupid and boring, for whatever reasons, was going to speak on campus, you probably would not attend. Conversely, if an individual for whom you had high regard was going to speak, you would be more likely to attend. Second, the view that you hold of a person before the influence situation will create a perceptual set, or expectation, predisposing you to either accept or reject evidence, agree or disagree, etc. Additionally, people excuse deficiencies on the part of those they regard as credible, whereas the same deficiencies found in those perceived as low-credible are viewed with exaggerated importance. Extrinsic source credibility is important. The sources to whom one exposes himself and the perceptual set with which an influence attempt is interpreted are both due to extrinsic source credibility.

Intrinsic factors of source credibility include all of the aspects of the influence situation. An individual's view of another's credibility is always changing to take into consideration the immediate experience. Brooks and Scheidel (1968) demonstrated the fluidity of source credibility when they had students listen to a speech by Malcolm X arguing for black separatism. They divided the taped speech into eight sections and had the subjects rate the credibility of Malcolm X after each of the eight segments. Additionally, they got scores prior to the speech and at the conclusion of the speech. The results indicated that the audience's perception of the source changed a great deal during the speech (see Fig. 4–6).

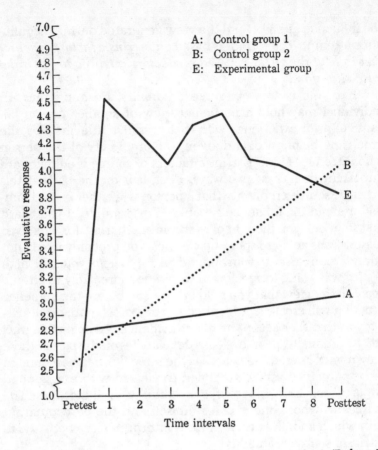

Fig. 4–6 Evaluative responses toward a source over time. (Robert D. Brooks and Thomas M. Scheidel, "Speech as Process: A Case Study," Speech Monographs, 35, 1, 1968, p. 4. Reprinted by permission.)

The intrinsic factors that account for such fluctuations in source credibility during an influence situation have been investigated extensively. We will examine the message characteristics of organization, evidence, language, and the delivery of the oral influence attempt.

Whether the influence attempt is a speech, a film, an ad, a tape, or whatever, it will have content. Seldom is the content presented in an entirely random fashion. Rather, some attempt is typically made to organize or structure the progression of ideas. Typical patterns of organization discussed in speech and English composition texts include chronological order, space order, problem-solution order, causal order, etc. Each of these organizational patterns reflects the expectation that people have learned through experience. Simply, we learn or come to expect that when someone begins speaking about the Civil War and first treats the events of the pre-War period, then 1861, then 1862, that 1863 will follow. When we read a description of England, we don't expect the text to jump from northwest England to southeast England to south central England, etc. Obviously, such expectations will affect the way we view those who violate or meet our expectations. Research has shown that the well-organized influence attempt may not cause an increase in the credibility of the source, but a disorganized message, a clear violation of expectation, will probably cause a decrease in the credibility of a source (Baker, 1965; McCroskey and Mehrley, 1969; Sharp and McClung, 1966).

Within the organized message two obvious components have received experimental investigation—evidence and language. McCroskey (1967; 1969) concluded that the moderate-to low-credible source is more effective if he uses evidence than if he does not, but that the high-credible source is no more persuasive when he uses evidence to support his assertions than when he does not. It appears that a source can be effective if he has (1) high credibility, or (2) moderate to low credibility and uses credible evidence. The high-credible source is already believable because of his credibility and does not need evidence. The low- or moderate-credible source, on the other hand, can improve his perceived credibility and his effectiveness by using highly credible evidence (Warren, 1969).

Two additional points about the use of evidence have been unearthed. First, when a moderate- or low-credible source uses evidence to improve the probability of his impact, he need not cite the source of the evidence or the qualifications of the source. Research has failed to support the common-sense notion that the source of evidence is a crucial factor (Cathcart, 1955; Bostrum and Tucker, 1969). Second, there is some reason to believe (Ostermeir, 1967) that in addition to using evidence from others to support an argument, a source can use his own experiences and knowledge (self-reference) as evidence. The frequency of self-reference by a source increases his perceived competence and, thus, the probability of influence.

Language use may also affect the perception of credibility. Obscenity, for instance, affects the dimensions of credibility. Specifically, obscenity increases perception of dynamism and decreases perception of trustworthiness, but its effects on competence are mixed (Baudhuin, 1971; Bostrum and Rossiter, 1969; Rodman, 1971). Other researchers (Bowers and Osborn, 1966; McEwen and Greenberg, 1970) have suggested that intense or metaphorical language results in increased perceived credibility of the user.

The delivery of oral influence attempts also affects source credibility and the probability of influence. Sereno and Hawkins (1967), for instance, explored the effects that nonfluencies (ah's, repetition, stuttering, etc.) have on credibility and found that the ratings of competence and dynamism decreased with an increasing number of nonfluencies, but that trustworthiness was unaffected. Miller and Hewgill (1964) found that vocalized pauses (e.g., "uh," "er") and repetition decreased the same dimensions. McCroskey and Mehrley (1969) found that fluency affected all dimensions. Apparently, the effects of delivery are additive (McCroskey, 1968); good delivery can increase credibility, and poor delivery can decrease it.

Source credibility is an extremely important factor affecting cue control NSI. Both extrinsic and intrinsic source credibility are in a continual state of fluctuation, and many of the variables causing this fluctuation are known. Many important variables affecting source credibility are probably not known at this time. Nevertheless, the importance of source credibility suggests this as an area of extensive future research.

SITUATIONAL FACTORS

A variety of factors of the specific situation affect the operation of cue control NSI. The first to be discussed is a conceptually imprecise and difficult one—the degree of external justification. Specifically, it has been the recurrent observation that an individual feels or perceives a greater magnitude of inconsistency to the extent that the external justification (force or reward) for doing so is low. In other words, to the extent that a person can rationalize his behavior ("he made me do it" or "I had to do it" or "I had no choice" or "I couldn't turn down the reward"), the perceived magnitude of inconsistency is minimal. Thus, felt inconsistency is greatest when behavior is the result of free choice or for which a person receives no reward. Imagine, for example, the difference you might experience in the following situations. If you heard a convincing speech that the college you attend is of extremely low quality and is about to lose its accreditation, you might well experience some inconsistency, especially if you were attending that school on your own choice and were receiving no reward for so doing. The full impact of the inconsistency would relate to you. What do you think would be your feeling if you were told by your family that they had all attended College X and if you wanted to go to school, you would attend College X. In addition, your rich aunt was paying you $1,000 a month for continuing at College X. In the latter circumstance, you could blame others for your attendance at a poor school, and the felt inconsistency would be less. In sum, the greater the situational external justification, the less the perceived magnitude of inconsistency.

Another factor of the situation is the perceived intent of the source. Though the research indicates that the perception of insincerity is improbable, Mills and Jellison (1968) demonstrated that when an audience does perceive the influencer as insincere or as having "an axe to grind," his effectiveness is reduced. Mills (1966), in another study, also showed that if a speaker is perceived as liking his audience, he will be more effective if the audience perceives that he desires to influence them than if he is not perceived as desiring influence. On the other hand, if the audience perceives that the source does not like them, he had better not show a desire to influence them. Clearly, the receiver's perception of the intention of the source is an important factor, but the nature and parameters of these effects are as yet unclear.

Five factors of the message have been shown to affect the probability or degree of influence. One of the earliest questions concerning message structure that research dealt with was the relative merits of presenting one-sided or two-sided speeches (Hovland, Janis, and Kelley, 1953; Lumsdaine and Janis, 1953). The question motivating this research was whether the influencer should just present his side or position on an issue or whether he should also present and refute the other side. A lot of research has subsequently been conducted (Bettinghaus and Basehart, 1969; McGinnies, 1966; Sears, 1966), and the conclusions that seem justified are:

1. A two-sided speech is more effective when
   a) the audience is intelligent
   b) the audience is initially opposed to the advocated position
   c) the audience is likely to hear the other side.
2. A one-sided speech is best advised when
   a) the audience is not intelligent
   b) the audience already agrees and is not likely to hear the other side.

Thus, the evidence suggests the general use of a two-sided speech. In today's world of mass information systems and the high probability of everyone hearing every side of any issue, a two-sided speech should almost be universal. Additionally, McGuire (1964) suggests that presentation and refutation of the opposing side provides the audience with a means of resisting later counterpersuasion.

Granted that a two-sided speech is advised, a number of other decisions become important. One decision is whether to treat your side first and then the other side, or vice-versa. Some research suggests that when an audience is initially unfamiliar with the issue, the pro side should be presented first, but when the audience is familiar, and especially familiar *and* opposed to the advocated position, the con side should be presented before the advocated position.

Another structural decision concerns the placement of the best evidence or argument. The question is: Should an argument build to a climax and rely on the impact of the temporally last item (recency), or should the best argument be presented first and the rest of the message be essentially anticlimactic, on the assumption that the first item will be remembered best and have the greatest impact (primacy)? There is yet a third organizational scheme, called the pyramidal order, in which the best argument is presented in the middle of the message. The issue apparently depends on a variety of situational factors (relevance of information, pleasantness of information, commitment), and the specification has yet to be made. Generally, we can conclude that the best argument or evidence should be at either the beginning or the end, but seldom, if ever, in the middle (Gulley and Berlo, 1956; Rosnow and Robinson, 1967).

When an argument is advanced, should the influencer explicitly draw the conclusion of the argument? For example, would it have been advisable for Dr. Testtube merely to indicate that eating fish is unhealthful, or should he have gone ahead to take the final step and assert that people ought not to eat fish? McGuire (1968) reviewed this entire issue and decided that except in unusual circumstances (extremely simple and familiar arguments or a time delay opportunity for the audience), the influencer should draw the conclusion.

Finally, the influencer has to decide how far away his position can be from that of the target(s). For example, if the audience is at position A on the topic of marijuana, could the influencer argue at position B or C or D? (See Fig. 4–7.)

MARIJUANA

Good D _ C _ B _ A Bad

Fig. 4–7 Three degrees of discrepancy (B, C, D) from an audience position (A).

Intuitively, at some degree of discrepancy the audience will reject the speaker and his argument. But every influencer wants to get as close as possible to that threshold in order to maximize influence. *Generally,* the greater the discrepancy advocated, the greater the change achieved. But the factors of issue clarity, source credibility, and ego-involvement affect this proposition. There is some evidence, for example, to suggest that large amounts of discrepancy will yield great change when the issue is clear, but that on an ambiguous issue, large amounts of discrepancy will "boomerang" and result in little influence. Similarly, the impact of source credibility on discrepancy is illustrated in Fig. 4–8, which shows that the high-credible source can "get away with" greater discrepancy, because he is less "derogatable" than the low- or moderate-credible source.

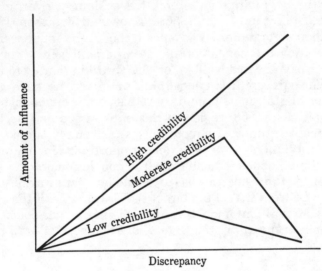

Fig. 4–8 *Effects of source credibility and discrepancy on amount of influence.*

Similarly, the ego-involvement of the audience will affect the perception of the amount of discrepancy and the degree of change a given discrepancy will produce. Specifically, the more ego-involved an individual is, the less discrepancy he will tolerate before he "boomerangs," and the less effective large amounts of discrepancy will be (Koslin, Stoops, and Loh, 1967; Zimbardo, 1960). This relationship is illustrated in Fig. 4–9.

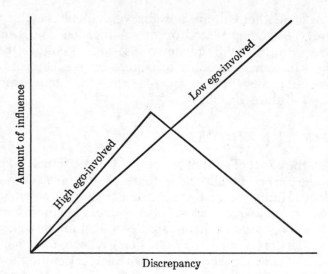

Fig. 4–9 *Effects of audience ego-involvement and discrepancy on amount of influence.*

CULTURAL FACTORS

The impact of culture on cue control is not yet well understood. Three effects, however, can be safely assumed. First, an individual's culture will affect the operation of cue control when the disposition elicited is an internalized cultural norm. Each culture will cause its members to internalize a different set of cultural norms. Accordingly, cues that may have been effective in producing influence in one culture may not be effective in another. Second, the disposition, or drive, for cognitive consistency may not be as strong or operate in the same manner from culture to culture. The evidence is very confusing to date, but there may be differences between oriental and occidental cultures in the importance of cognitive consistency. Finally, individuals of various cultures may be differentially sensitive to particular cues. For instance, persons of one culture may be more sensitive to particular cues. For example, persons of one culture may be more sensitive to cue A than to cue B than are persons of another culture. This difference could result from a greater value being placed on cue A than on cue B in one culture, or a greater frequency of use in one culture than in another. In short, the effect of culture on cue control is not known, but is thought to be an area worthy of intense research activity in future years.

BIOLOGICAL FACTORS

As with the effect of culture on cue control, not much is known about the effects of biological factors on cue control. Obviously, a biological limitation such as a hearing or vision problem would reduce an individual's sensitivity to cues. Furthermore, research in biological channel capacity and stimulus selectivity has implications for cue control. For instance, are people of different ages or sex differentially capable of attending to large numbers of cues? Are there biological reasons that some cues are more frequently attended to than others? These are seemingly important questions, but the research is not yet sufficiently advanced to support generalizations.

SUMMARY

NSI cue control occurs when the influencer provides cues that elicit predetermined responses from the receiver. Such responses are the result of dispositions within the receiver. Several types of dispositions are involved in cue control—internalized cultural norms, well-learned responses, expectations, and attitudes. The overriding disposition on which cue control relies is the desire to maintain cognitive consistency. Many psychological, sociological, and situational factors have been shown to affect the operation of cue control. Cultural and biological factors probably also affect cue control, but the effects are currently not understood.

Psychological Factors

1. *Cognitive consistency.* The more consistent the advocated premise is with the receiver's cognitive state, the greater the probability of acceptance.

2. *Credibility-proneness.* The higher the credibility-proneness of the target, the more susceptible he is to differences in source credibility.

3. *Authoritarianism and dogmatism.* The greater the authoritarianism or dogmatism of the target, the more susceptible he is to influence from an "authority."

4. *Tolerance for inconsistency.* The greater the target's tolerance for inconsistency, the less susceptible he is to influence.

   a) *Authoritarianism and dogmatism.* The greater an individual's authoritarianism or dogmatism, the lower his tolerance for inconsistency.

   b) *Anxiety.* The higher an individual's normal anxiety, the lower his tolerance for inconsistency.

   c) *Self-esteem.* The lower an individual's self-esteem, the lower his tolerance for inconsistency.

   d) *Ego-involvement.* The higher an individual's level of ego-involvement, the lower his tolerance for inconsistency.

5. *Effort.* An individual experiencing cognitive inconsistency will select the mode of resolution requiring the least effort, both immediate and long-term.

6. *Positivity bias.* The mode of inconsistency reduction involving change from negative to positive is more probable than is the mode of resolution involving cognitive changes from positive to negative.

Sociological Factors

1. *Source credibility.* As the perceived credibility of the influencer increases, the probability of influence increases.

   a) *Extrinsic credibility.* Extrinsic credibility affects the probability of a potential receiver's exposing himself to a particular message and, if he does, the perceptual set within which the message is interpreted.

   b) *Intrinsic credibility.* Intrinsic credibility is continually fluctuating and is determined by many factors.

1) *Message organization.* Well-organized messages do not necessarily increase perceived credibility, but disorganized messages probably do reduce perceived credibility.

2) *Evidence.* Highly credible sources may be effective without evidence, but low- and moderately credible sources will be perceived as more credible and more effective if they use evidence.

3) *Language.* Intense or metaphorical language may result in increased perceived credibility and effectiveness.

4) *Delivery.* "Good" delivery increases perceived credibility, and "poor" delivery decreases perceived credibility.

Situational Factors

1. *External justification.* The greater the external justification provided the target, the lower the probability of influence.

2. *Intent.* The perceived intent of the source affects the probability of influence.

3. *Message construction.* Many characteristics of the message (e.g., sidedness, conclusion-drawing, discrepancy, etc.) affect the probability of influence.

Cultural and Biological Factors

1. The effects of cultural and biological factors on cue control are as yet unspecified.

Chapter Five

When You are the Manipulator

On the basis of your reading of the previous chapters, you may have come to this point in your thinking about social influence: "O.K., so there are three general types of social influence, and each one is affected by a lot of different variables. What I want to know is, how can *I* influence other people (other than Clyde)?"

Fair question. Unfortunately, the current state of knowledge about social influence does not justify specific answers such as "Well, if you want to sell cars, get elected, or seduce your next date, you should always do X, Y, or Z." Such prescriptions are either unavailable or unreliable. Nevertheless, in this chapter we will explore the general strategies of social influence recommended by current understanding of the process.

SOCIAL INFLUENCE STRATEGY

Seldom is successful intentional influence the result of random or unplanned activity. Rather, successful influence attempts are based on a *strategy* for influence. A strategy is a general plan of action designed by the influencer to accomplish specific goals. For example, if you wished to move the proverbial obstinate mule, legend has it that you have two available strategies: the carrot or the stick. Specifically, you could induce movement by offering a carrot in front of the balky animal, or you could coerce action by applying a stick to the mule's backside. Once a particular strategy has been selected, specific *tactics* are developed to implement the general plan or strategy, e.g., how hard to hit the mule with the stick, or how far in front of the mule to place the carrot. Successful social influence requires attention to both strategy and tactics.

Although particular strategies developed for various situations appear to be quite different, successful influence strategies seem to be selected in a similar manner. That is, it is obvious that no single strategy will always be appropriate, but the general process of deciding which strategy would be most appropriate is understood. We will focus on this process of *deciding* how to influence rather than on how to influence.

Generally, successful influence strategies seem to be based on three factors: the influencer must (1) understand the social influence processes, (2) recognize the basic conditions of social influence as it operates in the "real world," and (3) determine strategy and select appropriate tactics based on an adequate situation analysis. The preceding chapters have provided the basis for understanding social influence processes. The basic conditions of social influence and a method of determining strategy and tactics will be covered in this chapter.

Basic Conditions of Social Influence

For successful influence strategy to be developed, the influencer must recognize some important aspects of social influence as it operates in the "real world." In addition to understanding social influence on a theoretical level or as it operates in the laboratory, the potential influencer must recognize and deal with the characteristics of social influence as he will actually attempt it—in a real situation with real people. Three of the more important factors or conditions of "real" social influence that must be recognized are:

1. the importance of the receiver

2. the limits on potential influence

3. the importance of a campaign approach to social influence.

Let's deal with each of these factors in turn.

Receiver Importance. If you attempted to influence another person and designed a strategy intended to make clear that if he complied with your expectations he would receive something he valued, the natural assumption would be that outcome control was operating. Though the assumption would be theoretically warranted, it might be wrong. The type of social influence that actually operates in any given situation is a function of the receiver's perception, not your intention. You may attempt outcome control and the receiver may view your behavior in the context of cue control or even ISI. For instance, many parents try to influence their children not to smoke (NSI), but smoke themselves. The child may be more influenced by their behavior (which would be ISI) than by their normative influence attempts, and therefore begin smoking. The receiver determines the type of influence that operates. The receiver confers or withholds credibility. The receiver is either effect dependent, information dependent, or both, or neither. The receiver will accept a premise or reject it. The receiver, in effect, creates the "real" message.

What the preceding illustrations emphasize is that even if you attempt outcome control NSI, it may be perceived as cue control or ISI. Thus, despite the fact that ISI is primarily the result of unintentional influence, the findings about ISI cannot be ignored when determining NSI strategy. It must always be remembered that ISI, outcome control, and cue control are theoretical distinctions that exist in textbooks; most real-life situations, however, have characteristics of ISI and both types of NSI operating simultaneously to some degree. In short, successful influence strategy must be based on a functional analysis of the forces operating on the target and not on a structural or psychological analysis of what the source does or what he intends.

Limits of Social Influence. Since "success" is determined by comparing the desired or anticipated change and the actual or achieved influence, strategies that overestimate potential influence or anticipate an unrealistic degree of influence are bound to be "unsuccessful." For example, Clyde's father, Senator Klutz, carried his state in the past presidential election. If Senator Klutz erroneously assumed that it was possible for him to win the presidential election, his campaign would have to be judged a "failure." If, on the other hand, the senator set a realistic goal of carrying one state as groundwork for a later presidential campaign, his campaign would be considered a "success." All attempts of social influence must be based on reasonable goals. Such a realistic prediction of possible influence is, however, predicated on a recognition of the limits of influence. Many factors discussed in earlier chapters ought to suggest that there are some very real and logical limits to the amount of influence that can be achieved in any given circumstance. Let's look at just a few of the reasons potential influence is limited.

First, the principle of cognitive consistency suggests that it is unlikely that people will even expose themselves to influence attempts that are extremely discrepant from their existing positions. Even if an individual were exposed to a wildly divergent view, he would probably distort his perception of it. How many John Birchers attend Democratic Party rallies? How many top-level defense employees read mail-outs from peace groups? Second, the research on ego-involvement demonstrates that as one's level of ego-involvement increases, the amount of influence accepted decreases. This research shows that only those low- or moderately ego-involved individuals are even susceptible to large amounts of influence. (How many such people are there?) Third, we found that the importance an individual places on various membership and reference groups and the value he places on the rewards they mediate is another factor limiting influence. Haven't you ever felt restrained from adopting a new attitude or changing your behavior because one of your reference or membership groups might not approve? Fourth, the sheer number of competing influence attempts precludes the possibility that any one influence attempt will have a primary determining effect. Is it reasonable to assume that a person will receive advertising messages from only one deodorant manufacturer? Fifth, we know that unless the opportunity to reinstate the source-message connection exists, the initial effects achieved as the result of high credibility will diminish over time. Finally, very real and pragmatic factors of the target's current state, such as time, money, or the possession of a car, pose obvious limits on his ability to be influenced. No matter how persuasive a Rolls-Royce salesman might be, I could not afford to buy one (unless this book sells five million copies). And the list of factors that limit potential influence goes on and on.

An accurate assessment of the limits to influence in a given situation is essential to the development of a successful strategy of influence. Indeed, an accurate assessment may even preclude trying to influence. Occasionally, one must admit that the amount of influence that can be reasonably anticipated is either zero or so slight as to be not worth the effort. Can you think of a combination of factors which would so severely restrict potential influence that it wouldn't be worth achieving? What about the person who is publicly committed to, and highly ego-involved in, a position for which he receives much social support and many rewards from other people? Is the Chief of Staff of the Army likely to become a peacenik? Is the president of the Great American Tobacco Company going to join an antismoking campaign?

Social influence involving real people on real issues is limited, and the recognition of limitations is crucial in designing an influence strategy if the influencer is to be as effective as the situation permits.

Campaign Approach to Social Influence. How often do you think important changes occur as the result of a single influence attempt? If you answered "seldom," you are probably right. Consider the circumstantial evidence. Advertisers spend millions of dollars in advertising campaigns. They use appeals that are repeated many times via many media. Can you imagine one of the major auto manufacturers advertising only once a year? Political candidates and evangelists are often able to personally speak in a given city only once, but they and their media advisers effectively use the media to reach the voter or potential convert before and after such appearances. The Communist brainwashing campaigns were characterized by Schein *et al.* (1961) as a three-step campaign consisting of unfreezing, changing, and refreezing stages. Sereno and Bodaken (1972) have found that for highly ego-involved audiences, "a program of persuasion may be necessary which incorporates strategies designed to produce gradual decreases in attitude of rejection along with concomitant increases in latitudes on noncommitment and acceptance. These changes would thus make an individual more susceptible for a subsequent change on his most acceptable position" (p. 158). Finally, your own experience probably supports a campaign view of successful influence; seduction, for example, is frequently a campaign. It may, depending on the circumstances, be a two-hour, three-date, ten-date,or even matrimonial campaign.

On the basis of these examples of "campaigns," it appears that a campaign is characterized by *stages*. That is, rather than simply attempting to accomplish the ultimate goal with a single strategy, a campaign has intermediate goals, each with its own strategy. In such a multistage influence attempt, each goal, up to and including the ultimate goal, builds on those preceding it. For example, as already indicated, reducing the level of ego-involvement is an important intermediate goal in influencing highly ego-involved audiences. Once that intermediate goal is accomplished, persuasion to a new position is possible.

Realistically, potential influencers must recognize and account for the superiority of influence campaigns over single-shot, single-strategy influence attempts. Whether the campaign is simple and of short duration (e.g., establishing credibility and then using that credibility to assist later influence attempts) or long-term and complex (e.g., using many media, many times to accomplish many intermediate goals), successful "real world" social influence is generally the result of well-designed influence campaigns.

In summary, if you desire to influence another individual, several characteristics of social influence as it operates in the real world are important to the design of your strategy. First, you must remember and account for the fact that the receiver of influence may not perceive your efforts as you intend. Second, you must recognize the limits of potential influence in any given situation in order to set realistic goals, whenever feasible. Once the basic conditions of social influence have been recognized, you are in a position to analyze the influence situation with which you are faced and to decide strategy and tactics.

Strategic and Tactical Decisions

The strategic and tactical decisions an influencer faces are numerous. All of these decisions are determined, either wholly or in part, on the basis of an analysis of the specific factors of the situation. Three of the most important decisions the influencer must make are:

1. What general strategy is most appropriate to the specific goals desired?
2. Will the social relationship between the influencer and the target support the strategy selected?

3. Which tactics will most effectively implement the selected strategy?

The influence strategy an individual chooses must be appropriate to the desired goal. Just as the decisions to hunt elephants with a .22 rifle or pheasants with a cannon are inappropriate strategy-goal combinations, an influencer can make seriously inappropriate decisions. An influencer must determine his specific goal precisely and then match that goal with an appropriate strategy. The use of an incorrect strategy to achieve a particular goal could result in either failure or the expenditure of more effort than was actually necessary. For example, the political candidate who tried to exercise outcome control on an audience ("You vote for me, or else"), is tempting fate and will probably remain a private citizen. Similarly, if a teacher wants Johnny to open a window, she need not develop a campaign to convince Johnny of the wisdom of opening the window; she need only tell him to do so. In very general terms, the following goal-strategy relationships seem apparent.

1. If all that is desired is mere compliance, NSI outcome control based on actual power is the most efficient strategy. For instance, if a parent wanted to influence a child to practice his French horn, a simple exchange of compliance for avoidance of punishment would be suggested. Similarly, an exchange of compliance and a promotion was effective in influencing Clyde's brother to shave off his beard.

Two serious limitations of this strategy exist, however. First, the behavior will probably persist only as long as the influencer has surveillance over the target (the child may stuff his French horn up the chimney the moment his parents leave for work) or as long as the target is actually effect dependent on the influencer (the beard may grow back if the boss is fired and a new, more lenient, boss is found). Second, the damage to the social relationship between the influencer and target is often serious (the child may hate his parents, as well as his French horn, and the employee may despise his overbearing boss). Thus, if you desire to establish or maintain a positive social relationship with the target, outcome control NSI by actual power may not be the best strategy. However, if compliance is all that is sought and the social relationship is irrelevant to you, outcome control NSI based on actual power is often the most efficient strategy.

2. If compliance is desired and the establishment or maintenance of a positive social relationship is important, NSI outcome control based on social power is an efficient strategy. The exchange of compliance and social rewards based on the relationship between the influencer and the target is common, e.g., Clyde cut his hair for social approval from his co-workers. This strategy may be more difficult to actually implement than that based on actual power, inasmuch as you may have to build the social relationship upon which you will ultimately trade. Nevertheless, compliance can be obtained from others who perceive you as similar, attractive, or likable. This strategy, however, also has some disadvantages that must be remembered.

Three characteristics of NSI outcome control based on social power limit its utility. First, there is a logical limit to the extent of influence or number of influence attempts a given social relationship can withstand. Simply, people will comply with a friend's wishes only so many times or to a certain extent. Once this threshold is reached or passed, of course, the influencer loses his base of influence and becomes functionally powerless ("I like him a lot, but this time he's gone too far. I simply won't do it!"). The second limitation to this strategy of influence relates to the first. Specifically, a precise determination of the target's evaluation of costs and rewards is necessary to carry out the strategy, but this is a very difficult task. A given receiver, for instance, may well be willing to exchange such behavioral compliance as telling a "little white lie" for you in order to obtain your gratitude, but that gratitude may not be sufficient to induce him to vote for a particular political candidate. The analysis requisite for this strategy is extensive, and because it is a subjective prediction, it is open to error. Finally, outcome control derived from social power may require surveillance for the continuation of the desired effect. Occasionally, the social relationship upon which an exchange is based is so strong that the target continues the desired behavior even in the absence of the influencer, but the persistence of the influence obtained from this strategy is questionable.

3.   Finally, if you want relatively permanent change without the necessity for continual surveillance and without giving something up as a reward, the strategy of cue control NSI is recommended. The impact of cue control takes place within the receiver, and because he rewards himself for being consistent with his own dispositions, the effect is relatively enduring. This strategy is also complex, however, as it requires extensive target analysis to determine the dispositions that can be made salient to achieve the desired goals. Furthermore, it is necessary to establish perceived credibility.

Clearly, the determination of a general strategy for influence must be based on a careful analysis of the specific goals desired. A few examples may illustrate the application of these guidelines.

* If you desired to convince a friend to register and vote Republican, you might reason as follows:

> The strategy of outcome control based on actual power would be ill-advised because the exercise of raw power may destroy our friendship and besides, what actual resource do I control? Furthermore, even if I were successful in persuading him to register as a Republican, I have no way of observing whether he votes Republican. Outcome control based on social power is similarly inappropriate. Though we are friends, it would be difficult to determine whether our friendship is strong enough to induce compliance. And again, even if I were successful, I would have no guarantee or check on compliance without surveillance. The strategy of cue control, however, appears appropriate. This strategy poses no threat to our friendship, does not "cost" me anything, and because he is my friend, I can reasonably predict the dispositions that can be cued or made salient. Furthermore, if I am successful, I can be confident that even those behaviors I can't observe will be consistent with my goal. Yes, the most appropriate strategy would be cue control.

- If you desired to persuade a person you knew only vaguely, and did not like, to take your place on a blind date with a person you discovered was an overbearing boor, your reasoning might go like this:

> Cue control probably isn't the best strategy. In the first place I would be hard-pressed to develop any credibility. Second, I don't know the target well enough to predict what dispositions can be made salient to accomplish my objective. Finally, the goal of avoiding the date isn't worth the work required to study the target, construct a message, and build some credibility. Outcome control by social power will not work either. There is no friendship to trade upon, and the target's evaluation of the proposed reward, my gratitude, is probably not very high. The strategy of outcome control by actual power makes sense. Obviously, I don't much care what the target thinks of me, and this strategy does not involve much work. Additionally, everybody is short of money and therefore places some value on that resource. That settles it; I'll pay him $15 to take my place on the date.

The preceding analysis indicates that a careful examination of the goal sought ought to give the influencer a good idea of the general strategy he should follow. Once a given strategy is decided upon, the question remains: "Will the social relationship between influencer and target support the selected strategy?" If, for example, one desires to exercise outcome control based on actual power, one must determine if indeed the target perceives himself effect dependent on the influencer. Similarly, for outcome control influence to occur because of social power, the source must be liked, attractive, or be perceived as similar to the target. Finally, for cue control influence to take place, the source must be perceived as credible. In short, each strategy, if it is to have any chance of being effective, must be supported by a particular relationship between the influencer and the target. If the influencer determines that the required relationship does not exist, the next question is: "Can the requisite relationship be developed?"

Obviously, for social influence to occur the strategy selected must be supported by the appropriate source-target relationship. If a source selected a strategy of outcome control by
actual power and the target did not perceive himself effect
dependent on the influencer, no influence could occur. Similarly, if an influencer chose cue control as his basic strategy, and
he was not viewed as credible and could not develop his credibility, little influence would occur. Regardless of the strategy
chosen, the influencer must carefully examine the social relationship to determine whether or not it will support the selected strategy. If it does not, he must redesign his strategy.

Once a particular strategy has been selected and the social
relationship has been deemed to support the selected strategy,
numerous tactical decisions must be faced. The following are
just a few of the decisions an influencer might face: How discrepant can the message be from the audience's initial position?
What social needs can be traded upon? How intense should the
language be? Which media should be used? How many messages are needed? How explicitly should the contingency be
presented? Should the conclusion be drawn or left to the audience? Whether to appear to desire influence or not? How large
a reward to offer for compliance? Answers to all such questions
must be reached as a result of a careful analysis of the specific
situation faced by the influencer. For example, the influencer
must determine some or all of the following: the audience's
attitudes, ego-involvement, credibility-proneness, attraction
for the source, evaluation of proposed rewards, perceived credibility of the source, sex, age, race, birth order, authoritarianism,
dogmatism, and degree of external justification. The propositions at the end of Chapters Two, Three, and Four should indicate the factors that would be relevant to these decisions. We
cannot cover all of the contingencies you may face as an influencer, but the following examples illustrate how these decisions are made.

If you have selected cue control as your general strategy
and need to decide the most effective degree of discrepancy,
the factors of ego-involvement, source credibility, and issue
clarity are known to be important. Specifically, if the audience
is highly ego-involved, the influencer is perceived as not very

credible, and the issue is ambiguous, very small amounts of discrepancy will be tolerated. On the other hand, if the audience has low ego-involvement in the issue, the influencer is perceived as highly credible, and the issue is clear, large amounts of discrepancy will probably produce large amounts of social influence. Thus, the determination of the specific tactic, message discrepancy, must be based on the situationally unique values on three variables.

If you selected outcome control based on social power as a strategy and wondered how much social approval to offer for compliance, several factors should be included in your determination. Specifically, less social approval would be required if the target had a high need for social approval or low self-esteem than if he had high self-esteem and was satiated on social approval. Furthermore, the degree of perceived similarity attraction or liking will affect the amount of social approval required.

Tactical decisions must be based on a careful analysis of the specific situation with which the influencer is faced; no one tactic is always appropriate. The quality and effectiveness of an individual's strategic and tactical decisions will be a measure of his knowledge of social influence processes, recognition of the basic conditions of social influence, and analysis of the influence situation. Were social influence a "science," achieving maximum potential influence would be a matter of course. However, social influence is still an "art," and success is contingent upon the influencer's ability to apply the appropriate generalizations to the unique situation. Such ability comes only through knowledge and experience.

Strategic and Tactical Decisions: Another Dimension. To this point we have been discussing the decisions an influencer must make in order to be effective. However, the power to persuade, like political power, ought not be handed over to individuals who do not recognize the responsibilities associated with such power. Just as we applaud politicians who use their power to the benefit of their constituents and impeach, or ought to impeach, those who use their power for personal gain, we make ethical judgments of others' use of the power of social influence.

Clearly, there are occasions when a strategy or tactic might be effective but not desirable or ethical: a gun to a person's head is likely to be effective in inducing compliance; lying is often an effective persuasive tactic; and physical torture is a universally efficient technique of influence. Though few would deny the effectiveness of such procedures, most condemn them as unethical. Similarly, the exercise of social influence to achieve goals contrary to the best interest of the receiver is regarded as ethically suspect. A salesman, for instance, who is effective in persuading a customer to purchase a product known to be inferior or overpriced is viewed by many as ethically reprehensible.

Fortunately, our society has recognized the power of social influence and its potentially unethical uses. Accordingly, we have laws governing the use of social influence in the public domain, e.g., truth in advertising, slander, libel, and campaign practices laws. However, in many areas of day-to-day exchange no such laws exist, and a critical and informed populace is our only protection. It is beyond the scope of this book to survey all the possible criteria for making ethical distinctions or all the situations in which such decisions must be made. However, the recognition of the responsibility attendant to the power of social influence is the important first step toward discovering the ethical guidelines which will govern your own social influence behavior and with which you will judge others' attempts at social influence.

Resistance

Let's assume that you have identified the goals you desire, decided on an appropriate strategy, found the relationship between yourself and the target to be supportive of the chosen strategy, analyzed the situation and the target, determined specific tactics, and that your campaign was successful. What guarantee do you have that the influence you had on the target's attitudes, beliefs, or behavior will persist? None! The next obvious question is: "Is there anything an influencer can do to increase the probability that his influence will persist?" Yes, there appear to be some tentative suggestions concerning techniques of making an audience resistant to later counterpersuasion. Before we explore those recommendations, however, an example may illustrate the need for being concerned about making an audience resistant to persuasion.

In a small town in Montana, two politicians were running for mayor: Mr. Good and Mr. Wellspoken. They were partners in a gas station. A town meeting was held every Friday night, and most of the townspeople attended these meetings during the months prior to the election. However, because the partners did not want to lose the lucrative gasoline business from the nearby interstate freeway, only one of the candidates could go to the Friday night meetings, while the other one pumped gas. So they took turns going to the meetings and speaking to the assembled voters.

The undertaker's son, a graduate student in communication, was studying the mayoral election and took opinion polls every Saturday morning. After a few weeks his results showed a curious pattern:

	Mr. Wellspoken	Mr. Good
Sept. 21	59%	41%
Sept. 28	40%	60%
Oct. 5	58%	42%
Oct. 12	41%	59%
Oct. 19	58%	42%

Apparently, each candidate was very effective on Friday night, but his influence lasted only until the next Friday night, when his equally effective opponent spoke at the town meeting. Ultimately, neither candidate was elected; they fought so hard to determine who would speak on the last Friday evening before the election that they were both arrested on felony assault charges and declared ineligible for office by the justice of the peace, whose wife won the election with a strong write-in vote.

Obviously, each candidate was influential. One or the other would have won the election had he been able to not only influence his targets, but also to make them resistant to the later counterpersuasion of his opponent. How can that be done?

McGuire (1962, 1964) has developed a means of providing resistance to persuasion. He reasoned that an influencer could "innoculate" his audience against later counterpersuasion by providing either *supportive defenses* or *refutational defenses*. A supportive defense bolsters belief in the advocated position by providing for the audience the reasoning, evidence, or argument that supports the belief. A refutational defense is provided when an influencer explains and refutes the arguments against the position he is advocating. For example, if I wanted to convince you that we should have extensive federal aid to colleges, I could provide supportive defense by giving you as much evidence, argument, or reasoning as possible to bolster your belief in federal aid to colleges. Refutational defenses against later counterpersuasion could be provided by telling you of the arguments of those opposed to federal aid to colleges and demonstrating how these arguments can be refuted or countered.

Audiences provided with either type of defense are less susceptible to influence from another source than are audiences not provided with such defenses. Obviously, a combination of types of defenses is superior to either one alone (McGuire and Papegorgis, 1961; McGurrin, 1972). Though this technique has been employed primarily with noncontroversial topics, some research has shown that these resistance-producing techniques can be used with controversial issues as well (Brown, 1972; Ray, 1967).

In short, an influence campaign that seeks relatively enduring effects and does not attempt to make the targets resistant to the inevitable counterpersuasion they will receive at some later time is going to be of limited effectiveness. Accordingly, though the research on credibility and evidence may indicate that a high-credible source need not use or cite evidence, he may desire to use and cite the source of evidence to provide supportive defenses for his audiences. Unfortunately, the research is not currently sufficient to provide simple and realistic suggestions concerning resistance. However, it is both intuitively obvious and empirically supported that if an influence campaign is to have any lasting effect, the influencer must consider what his audience is going to be exposed to when they leave him. To think resistance to counterpersuasion not important is naive. To not attempt to provide such resistance is folly.

SUMMARY

So you want to sell cars? Get a promotion? Be respected by your peers? Convert your boyfriend or girlfriend to sexual liberalism? And you want to know how to accomplish these lofty objectives? Because not all car buyers, employers, peers, or dates are the same, no single influence practice can be recommended. Rather, we know that the influencer must:

1. Understand social influence processes
2. Recognize the basic conditions of social influence
   a) the importance of the receiver
   b) the limits to influence
   c) the importance of a campaign approach
3. Determine social influence strategy
   a) determine goal(s)
   b) match strategy to goal(s)
   c) determine that the social relationship between source and target will support the selected strategy
4. Determine tactics
   a) analyze the target(s) and situation
   b) select the tactics appropriate to resultant analysis
5. Provide a basis for the target(s)' resistance to later counter-persuasion.

Will you necessarily be an effective influencer if you follow each of these steps? Probably not. Despite the amount of research currently available, social influence is still an art, not a science. Will following these steps increase the probability of being influential? Yes! And in this improbable world, that is all one can expect, unless he is persuaded otherwise.

References

Abelson, R. P., E. Aronson, W. J. McGuire, T. M. Newcomb, M. J. Rosenberg, P. H. Tannenbaum, eds., *Theories of Cognitive Consistency: A Sourcebook,* Chicago: Rand McNally, 1968.

Adams, J. S. "Inequity in social exchange," in L. Berkowitz, ed., *Advances In Experimental Social Psychology,* Vol. 2, New York: Academic Press, 1964, pp. 267–299.

Adams, J. S. "A framework for the study of modes of resolving inconsistency," in Abelson *et al.,* eds., *Theories of Cognitive Consistency: A Sourcebook, op. cit.,* pp. 655–660.

Ajzen, I., and M. Fishbein, "The prediction of behavior from attitudinal and normative variables," in C. D. Mortenson and K. K. Sereno, eds., *Advances In Communication Research,* New York: Harper & Row, 1973, pp. 71–77.

Allen, V. L., and J. M. Levine, "Social support and conformity: The role of independent assessment of reality," *J. Exp. Soc. Psych.,* **7** (1971): 48–58.

Allport, G. W., "Attitudes," in M. Fishbein, ed., *Readings In Attitude Theory and Measurement,* New York: John Wiley, 1967, pp. 3–13.

Archibald, W. P, and R. L. Cohen, "Self-presentation, embarrassment, and facework as a function of self-evaluation, conditions of self-preservation, and feedback from others," *J. Pers. Soc. Psych.* **20** (1971): 287–297.

Argyle, M., "Social pressure in public and private situations," *J. Abnorm. Soc. Psych.* **54** (1957): 172–175.

Aronson, E., *The Social Animal,* San Francisco: W. H. Freeman, 1972.

Aronson, E., and B. W. Golden, "The effects of relevant and irrelevant aspects of communicator credibility on opinion change," *J. of Pers.* **30** (1962): 115–136.

Aronson, E., "Dissonance theory: Progress and problems," in Abelson *et al.,* eds., *Theories of Cognitive Consistency: A Sourcebook, op. cit.,* pp. 5–27. (a)

Aronson, E., "Discussion: Expectancy vs. other motives," in Abelson *et al.,* eds., *Theories of Cognitive Consistency: A Sourcebook, op. cit.,* pp. 491–494. (b)

Back, K. W., and K. E. Davis, "Some personal and situational factors relevant to the consistency and prediction of conforming behavior," *Sociometry,* **28** (1965): 227–240.

Baker, E. E., "The immediate effects of perceived speaker disorganization on speaker credibility and audience attitude change in persuasive speaking," *Western Speech,* **29** (1965): 148–161.

Bandura, A., *Psychological Modeling: Conflicting Theories*, Chicago: Aldine-Atherton, Inc., 1971.

Bandura, A., and A. C. Huston, "Identification as a process of incidental learning," *J. Abnorm. Soc. Psych.*, 63 (1961): 311–318.

Bandura, A., D. Ross, and S. A. Ross, "A comparative test of the status envy, social power, and secondary reinforcement theories of identificatory learning," *J. Abnorm. Soc. Psych.*, 67 (1963): 527–534.

Bandura, A., "Behavioral modifications through modeling procedures," in L. Krasner and L. P. Ullmann, eds., *Research In Behavior Modification*, New York: Holt, Rinehart and Winston, 1965, pp. 310–340.

Barnlund, D. C., "Communication: The context of change," in C. E. Larson, and F. E. Dance, eds., *Perspectives On Communication*, Milwaukee: Speech Communication Center, 1968, pp. 24–40.

Baron, R. A., "Reducing the influence of an aggressive model: The restraining effects of discrepant modeling cues," *J. Pers. Soc. Psych.*, 20 (1971): 240–245.

Basehart, J. R., "Message opinionation and approval-dependence as determinants of receiver attitude change and recall," *Speech Monographs*, 4 (1971): 302–310.

Bass, B. M., "Development and evaluation of a scale for measuring social acquiescence," *J. Abnorm. Soc. Psych.*, 53 (1956): 296–299.

Baudhuin, E. S., "Obscene language and source credibility: An experimental study," Paper presented to the International Communication Association, April 1971.

Bauer, R., "Communication as a transaction: A comment on "On the concept of influence," *Public Opinion Quarterly*, 27 (1963): 83–86.

Becker, S., and J. Carroll, "Ordinal position and conformity," *J. Abnorm. Soc. Psych.*, 65 (1962): 129–131.

Bell, P. R., "Publicity of initial decisions and the risky shift phenomenon," *J. Exp. Soc. Psych.*, 6 (1970): 329–345.

Beloff, H., "Two forms of social conformity: Acquiescence and conventionality," *J. Abnorm. Soc. Psych.*, 56 (1958): 99–104.

Bem, D. J., *Beliefs, Attitudes, and Human Affairs*, Belmont, Calif.: Brooks/Cole, 1970.

Berelson, B., P. F. Lazarfeld, and W. W. McPhee, *"Voting: A Study of Opinion Function During A Presidential Campaign,"* Chicago: University of Chicago Press, 1954.

Berenda, R. W., *The Influence of the Group On the Judgments of Children: An Experimental Investigation,* New York: Kings Crown Press, 1950.

Berlo, D., *The Process of Communication: An Introduction to Theory and Practice,* New York: Holt, Rinehart and Winston, 1960.

Berlyne, D. E., *Conflict, Arousal, and Curiosity,* New York: McGraw-Hill, 1960.

Berne, E., *Games People Play: The Psychology of Human Relationships,* New York: Grove Press, 1964.

Bettinghaus, E. P., and J. R. Basehart, "Some specific factors affecting attitude change," *J. of Communication,* 19 (1969): 227–238.

Bettinghaus, E. P., G. Miller, and T. Steinfatt, "Source evaluation, syllogistic content, and judgments of logical validity by high- and low-dogmatic persons," *J. Pers. Soc. Psych.,* 16 (1970): 238–244.

Bickman, L., "Social influence and diffusion of responsibility in an emergency," *J. Exp. Soc. Psych.,* 8 (1972): 438–445.

Blau, P. M., "Patterns of deviation in work groups," *Sociometry,* 23 (1960): 245–261.

Blau, P. M., *Exchange and Power In Social Life,* New York: John Wiley, 1964.

Bochner, S., and C. Insko, "Communicator discrepancy, source credibility, and influence," *J. Pers. Soc. Psych.,* 4 (1966): 614–621.

Bostrum, R. N., and R. K. Tucker, "Evidence, personality, and attitude change," *Speech Monographs,* 36 (1969): 22–27.

Bostrum, R. N., and G. Rossiter, "Profanity, justification, and source credibility," Paper presented to the International Communication Association, 1969.

Bowers, J. W., and M. M. Osborn, "Attitudinal effects of selected types of concluding metaphors in persuasive speeches," *Speech Monographs,* 33 (1966): 147–155.

Bramel, D., "Dissonance, expectation, and the self," in Abelson *et al.,* eds., *Theories of Cognitive Consistency: A Sourcebook,* Chicago: Rand McNally, 1968, pp. 355–365.

Brigante, T. R., "Adolescent evaluation of rewarding, neutral, and punishing power figures," *J. of Pers.,* 26 (1958): 435–450.

Britt, D. W., "Effects of probability of reinforcement and social stimulus consistency on imitation," *J. Pers. Soc. Psych.,* 18 (1971): 189–200.

Brock, T., "Implications of commodity theory for value change," in G. Greenwald, T. C. Brock, and T. M. Ostrom, eds., *Psychological Foundations of Attitudes*, New York: Academic Press, 1968, pp. 243–276.

Brockreide, W. E., "Dimensions of the concept of rhetoric," in K. K. Sereno, and C. D. Mortenson, *Foundations of Communication Theory*, New York: Harper & Row, 1970, pp. 25–39.

Brooks, R. D., and T. M. Scheidel, "Speech as process: A case study," *Speech Monographs*, 35 (1968): 1–7.

Brown, B. R., "Face saving following experimentally induced embarrassment," *J. Exp. Soc. Psych.*, 6 (1970): 255–271.

Brown, B. R., "Saving face," *Psych. Today*, 4 (1971): 55–59.

Brown, B. R., and H. Garland, "The effects of incompetency, audience acquaintanceship, and anticipated evaluative feedback on face-saving behavior," *J. Exp. Soc. Psych.*, 7 (1971): 490–502.

Brown, C. L., "Intervening variables in resistance to persuasion," Doctoral Dissertation: University of Calif., Davis; Ann Arbor, Michigan: Xerox University Microfilms, 1972, No. 72–9878.

Brown, R., *Social Psychology*, New York: The Free Press, 1965.

Bruner, J. S., and L. Postman, "On the perception of incongruity," in M. D. Vernon, ed., *Experiments In Visual Perception*, Baltimore: Penguin Books, 1966, pp. 285–292.

Buck, J., "The effects of negro and white dialectal variations upon attitudes of college students," *Speech Monographs*, 35 (1968): 181–186.

Burgoon, M., G. Miller, and S. Tubbs, "Machiavellianism, justification, and attitude changes following CAA," *J. Pers. Soc. Psych.*, 22 (1972): 366–371.

Burnstein, E., "Sources of cognitive bias in the representation of simple social structures: Balance, minimal change, positivity, reciprocity, and the respondent's own attitude," *J. Pers. Soc. Psych.*, 7 (1967): 36–48.

Calder, B. J., M. Ross, and C. Insko, "Attitude change and attitude attribution: effects of incentive, choice, and consequences," *J. Pers. Soc. Psych.*, 25 (1973): 84–99.

Carment, D. W., "Ascendant-submissive behavior in pairs of human subjects as a function of their emotional responsiveness and opinion strength," *Canadian J. Psych.*, 15 (1961): 45–51.

Carrigan, W. C., and J. W. Julian, "Sex and birth order differences in conformity as a function of need affiliation arousal." *J. Pers. Soc. Psych.,* 3 (1966): 479–483.

Cathcart, R. S., "An experimental study of the relative effectiveness of four methods of presenting evidence," *Speech Monographs,* 22 (1955): 227–233.

Centers, R., R. W. Shomer, and A. Rodrigues, "A field experiment in interpersonal persuasion using authoritative influence," *J. of Pers.,* 38 (1970): 392–403.

Coleman, J., "Comment on "On the concept of influence," *Public Opinion Quarterly,* 27 (1963): 63–82.

Cottrell, N. B., "Performance in the presence of other human beings: Mere presence, audience, and affiliation effects," in E. C. Simmel, R. A. Hoppe, and G. A. Milton, eds., *Social Facilitation and Imitative Behavior,* Boston: Allyn and Bacon, 1968, pp. 91–110.

Croner, M. D., and R. W. Willis, "Perceived differences in task competence and asymmetry of dyadic influence," *J. Abnorm. Soc. Psych.,* 62 (1961): 705–708.

Crooks, J. L., "Observational learning of fear in monkeys," unpublished manuscript, University of Pennsylvania, 1967.

Crowne, D. P., and S. Leverant, "Conformity under varying conditions of personal commitment," *J. Abnorm. Soc. Psych.,* 66 (1963): 547–555.

Crutchfield, R. S., "Conformity and character," *American Psychologist,* 10 (1955): 191–198.

Dabbs, J. M., and H. Leventhal, "Effects of varying recommendations in a fear-arousing communication," *J. Pers. Soc. Psych.,* 4 (1966): 525–531.

Darley, J. M., "Fear and social comparison as determinants of conformity behavior," *J. Pers. Soc. Psych.,* 4 (1966): 73–78.

Dashiell, J. F., "An experimental analysis of some group effects," *J. Abnorm. Soc. Psych.,* 25 (1930): 190–199.

Dashiell, J. F., "Experimental studies of the influence of social situations on the behavior of individual human adults," in C. Murchison, ed., *A Handbook of Social Psychology,* Vol. 2, New York: Russell, 1935, pp. 1097–1158.

Deaux, K., "Anticipatory attitude change: A direct test of the self-esteem hypothesis," *J. Exp. Soc. Psych.,* 8 (1972): 143–155.

Deutsch, M., and H. Gerard, "A study of normative and informational social influences upon individual judgment," *J. Abnorm. Soc. Psych.,* 51 (1955): 629–36.

Dinner, S. H., B. E. Lewkowicz, and J. Cooper, "Anticipatory attitude change as a function of self-esteem and issue familiarity," *J. Pers. Soc. Psych.*, 24 (1972): 407–412.

Dittes, J. E., and H. H. Kelley, "Effects of different conditions of acceptance upon conformity to group norms," *J. Abnorm. Soc. Psych.*, 53 (1956): 100–107.

Di Vesta, F. J., "Effects of confidence and motivation on susceptibility to informational social influences," *J. Abnorm. Soc. Psych.*, 59 (1959): 204–209.

Di Vesta, F. J., and J. C. Merwin, "The effects of need-oriented communications on attitude change," *J. Abnorm. Soc. Psych.*, 60 (1960): 80–85.

Doob, A. N., and A. E. Gross, "Status of frustrator as an inhibitor of horn-honking responses," *J. Soc. Psych.*, 76 (1968): 213–218.

Doob, L. W., "The behavior of attitudes," In M. Fishbein, ed., *Readings In Attitude Theory and Measurement,* New York: John Wiley, 1967, pp. 42–50.

Duncker, K., "Experimental modifications of children's food preferences through social suggestion," *J. Abnorm. Soc. Psych.*, 33 (1938): 489–507.

Ehrlich, D., J. Guttman, P. Schonbach, and J. Mills, "Postdecision exposure to relevant information," *J. Abnorm. Soc. Psych.*, 54 (1957): 98–102.

Emerson, R. M., "Power-dependence relations," *American Sociological Review,* 27 (1962): 31–41.

Endler, N., "Conformity as a function of different reinforcement schedules," *J. Pers. Soc. Psych.*, 4 (1966): 175–180.

Erickson, M. T., "Effects of social deprivation and satiation on verbal conditioning in children," *J. Comp. Physio. Psych.*, 55 (1962): 953–957.

Eskola, A., *Social Influence and Power In Two-Person Groups,* Copenhagen: Munksgaard Publishers, 1961.

Ettinger, R., C. J. Marino, and N. S. Endler, "Effects of agreement and correctness on relative competence and conformity," *J. Pers. Soc. Psych.*, 19 (1971): 204–212.

Feather, N. T., "Acceptance and rejection of arguments in relation to attitude strength, critical ability, and intolerance of inconsistency," *J. Abnorm. Soc. Psych.*, 69 (1964): 127–136.

Festinger, L., "Informal social communication," *Psych. Rev.,* 57 (1950): 271–282.

Festinger, L., "A theory of social comparison process," *Human Relations,* **7** (1954): 117–140.

Festinger, L., *A Theory of Cognitive Dissonance,* Stanford: Stanford University Press, 1957.

Festinger, L., "An analysis of compliant behavior," in M. Sherif and M. O. Wilson, eds., *Group Relations At the Crossroads,* New York: Harper & Row, 1953, pp. 232–256.

Festinger, L., and J. Thibaut, "Interpersonal communication in small groups," *J. Abnorm. Soc. Psych.* **46** (1951): 92–99.

Fiedler, F. E., and W. A. T. Meuwese, "Leader's contribution to task performance in cohesive and uncohesive groups," *J. Abnorm. Soc. Psych.,* **67** (1963): 83–86.

Fishbein, M., "A consideration of beliefs, and their role in attitude measurement," in M. Fishbein, ed., *Readings in Attitude Theory and Measurement,* New York: John Wiley, 1967, pp. 257–266.

Fishbein, Martin, ed., *Readings in Attitude Theory and Measurement.* New York: John Wiley, 1967.

Fishbein, M., "The prediction of behaviors from attitudinal variables," in C. D. Mortensen and K. K. Sereno, eds., *Advances In Communication Research,* New York: Harper & Row, 1973, pp. 3–31.

Fotheringham, W. C., *Perspectives On Persuasion,* Boston: Allyn and Bacon, 1966.

Foulkes, D., and S. H. Foulkes, "Self-concept, dogmatism, and tolerance of trait inconsistency," *J. Pers. Soc. Psych.,* **2** (1965): 104–111.

Fowler, H., *Curiosity and Exploratory Behavior,* New York: Macmillan, 1965.

Fraser, R., "Conformity and anticonformity in Japan," *J. Pers. Soc. Psych.,* **15** (1970): 203–210.

French, J. R. and B. H. Raven, "The bases of social power," in D. Cartwright ed., *Studies in Social Power,* Ann Arbor, Michigan: Institute for Social Research, 1959, pp. 150–167.

French, J. R., and R. S. Snyder, "Leadership and interpersonal power," in D. Cartwright, ed., *Studies in Social Power,* Ann Arbor, Michigan: Institute for Social Research, 1959, pp. 118–149.

Frye, R. L., and B. M. Bass, "Behavior in a group related to tested social acquiescence," *J. Soc. Psych.,* **61** (1963): 263–266.

Gamson, W. A., "Experimental studies of coalition formation," in L. Berkowitz, ed., *Advances in Experimental Social Psychology,* Vol. 1, New York: Academic Press, 1964, pp. 82–110.

Gerard, H. B., "Conformity and commitment to the group," *J. Abnorm. Soc. Psych.*, 68 209–211.

Gerard, H. B., R. A. Wilhelmy, and E. S. Conolley, "Conformity and group size," *J. Pers. Soc. Psych.*, 8 (1968): 79–82.

Gewirtz, J. L., and D. M. Baer, "The effect of brief social deprivation on behaviors for a social reinforcer," *J. Abnorm. Soc. Psych.*, 56 (1958): 49–56.

Goffman, E., "On face-work: An analysis of ritual elements in social interaction," in C. Gordon and K. Gergen, eds., *The Self In Social Interaction*, Vol. 1, New York: John Wiley, 1968, pp. 309–325.

Goldberg, S. C., and A. Lubin, "Influence as a function of perceived judgment error," *Human Relations*, 11 (1958): 275–280.

Gordon, G., *Persuasion: The Theory and Practice of Manipulative Communication*, New York: Hastings House, 1971.

Gray, L. N., J. T. Richardson and B. H. Mayhew, "Influence attempts and effective power: A re-examination of an unsubstantiated hypothesis," *Sociometry*, 31 (1968): 245–258.

Greenwald, A. G., T. C. Brock, and T. M. Ostrom, *Psychological Foundations of Attitudes*, New York: Academic Press, 1968.

Gruder, C. L., "Social power in interpersonal negotiation," in P. Swingle, ed., *The Structure of Conflict*, New York: Academic Press, 1970, pp. 111–154.

Grusec, J. E., "Some antecedents of self-criticism," *J. Pers. Soc. Psych.*, 4 (1966): 244–252.

Gulley, H. E., and D. K. Berlo, "Effect of intercellular and intracellular speech structure on attitude change and learning," *Speech Monographs*, 23 (1956): 288–297.

Hass, R. G., and D. E. Linden, "Counter argument availability and the effect of message structure in persuasion," *J. Pers. Soc. Psych.*, 23 (1972): pp. 219–233.

Hastorf, A. H., D. J. Schneider, and J. Polefka, *Person Perception*, Reading, Mass: Addison-Wesley, 1970.

Heider, F., "Attitudes and cognitive organization," *J. Psych.*, 21 (1946): 107–112.

Heider, F., *The Psychology of Interpersonal Relations*, New York: John Wiley, 1958.

Henchy, T., and D. C. Glass, "Evaluation apprehension and the social facilitation of dominant and subordinate responses," *J. Pers. Soc. Psych.*, 10 (1968): 446–454.

Hollander, E. P., "Conformity, status, and idiosyncrasy credit," *Psych. Rev.*, **65** (1958): 117–127.

Homans, G. C., *Social Behavior: Its Elementary Forms*, New York: Harcourt Brace and World, 1961.

Hornstein, H. A., M. Deutsch, and B. A. Benedict, "Compliance to threats directed against self and against an innocent third person," Technical Report No. 6, 1966, Office of Naval Research.

Horowitz, I. A., "Attitude change as a function of perceived arousal," *J. Soc. Psych.*, **87** (1972): 117–126.

Hovland, C., and W. Weiss, "The influence of source credibility on communication effectiveness," *Pub. Opin. Quart.*, **15** (1951): 635–650.

Hovland, C., I. L. Janis, and H. H. Kelley, *Communication and Persuasion: Psychological Studies of Opinion Change*, New Haven: Yale University Press, 1953.

Hurwitz, J., A. Zander, and B. Hymovitch, "Some effects of power on the relations among group members," in D. Cartwright and A. Zander, eds., *Group Dynamics: Research and Theory*, 3rd ed., New York: Harper & Row, 1968, pp. 291–297.

Insko, C. A., *Theories of Attitude Change*, New York: Appleton-Century-Crofts, 1967.

Iscoe, I., and M. S. Williams, "Experimental variables affecting the conformity behavior of children," *J. Pers.*, **31** (1963): 234–246.

Jackson, J. M., and H. D. Saltzstein, "The effect of person-group relationships on conformity processes," *J. Abnorm. Soc. Psych.*, **57** (1958): 17–24.

Jacobson, W. D., *Power and Interpersonal Relations*, Belmont, Calif.: Wadsworth, 1972.

Janis, I. L., "Anxiety indices related to susceptibility to persuasion," *J. Abnorm. Soc. Psych.*, **51** (1955): 663–667.

Johnson, H. H., J. M. Torcivia, and M. A. Poprick, 'Effects of source credibility on the relationship between authoritarianism and attitude change," *J. Pers. Soc. Psych.*, **9** (1968): 179–183.

Jones, E. E., *Ingratiation: A Social Psychological Analysis*, New York: Appleton-Century-Crofts, 1964.

Jones, E. E., and H. B. Gerard, *Foundations of Social Psychology*, New York: John Wiley, 1967.

Jones, E. E., K. J. Gergen, and R. G. Jones, "Tactics of ingratiation among leaders and subordinates in a status hierarchy," *Psych. Mono.*, **77** (3, whole No. 566) 1963.

Jones, E. E., and R. G. Jones, "Optimum conformity as an ingratiation tactic," *J. Pers.*, **32** (1964): 436–458.

Jones, R. A., and J. W. Brown, "Persuasiveness of one-and two-sided communications as a function of awareness there are two sides," *J. Exp. Soc. Psych.*, **6** (1970): 47–56.

Katz, E., and P. F. Lazarsfeld, *Personal Influence; The Part Played By People in the Flow of Mass Communications*, Glencoe, Ill.: Free Press, 1965.

Kelman, H., "Processes of opinion change," *Pub. Opin. Quart.*, **25** (1961): 57–78.

Kelman, H., and C. I. Hovland, "Reinstatement of the communicator in delayed measurement of opinion change," *J. Abnorm. Soc. Psych.*, **48** (1953): 327–335.

Kidder, L., and P. Brickman, "When directness is the better part of valor: Effects of normative and informational pressure on direct and indirect attitude tests," *J. Pers. Soc. Psych.*, **18** (1971): 238–246.

Kiesler, C. A., and S. B. Kiesler, *Conformity*, Reading, Mass.: Addison-Wesley, 1969.

Kipnis, D., "The effects of leadership style and leadership power upon the inducement of an attitude change," *J. Abnorm. Soc. Psych.*, **57** (1958): 173–180.

Kogan, N., and M. A. Wallach, "Group risk taking as a function of members' anxiety and defensiveness," *J. Pers.*, **35** (1967): 50–63.

Koslin, B. L., J. W. Stoops, and W. D. Loh, "Source characteristics and communication discrepancy as determinants of attitude change and conformity," *J. Exp. Soc. Psych.*, **3** (1967): 230–242.

Landy, D., "The effects of an overheard audience's reaction and attractiveness on opinion change," *J. Exp. Soc. Psych.*, **8** (1972): 276–288.

Latané, B., and J. M. Darley, *The Unresponsive Bystander: Why Doesn't He Help?* New York: Appleton-Century-Crofts, 1970.

Latané, B., and J. Rodin, "A lady in distress: Inhibiting effects of friends and strangers on bystander intervention," *J. Exper. Soc. Psych.*, **5** (1969): 189–202.

League, B. J., and D. N. Jackson, "Conformity, veridicality, and self-esteem," *J. Pers. Soc. Psych.*, **6** (1964): 113–115.

Le Bon, G., *The Crowd*, London: Unwin, 1896 (trans. from *Psychologies des Foules*, Paris: Oleon, 1895).

Lefkowitz, M., R. R. Blake, and J. S. Mouton, "Status factors in pedestrian violation of traffic signals," *J. Abnorm. Soc. Psych.*, **51** (1955): 704–706.

Leventhal, H., R. Singer, and S. Jones, "The effects of fear and specificity of recommendations upon attitudes and behavior," *J. Pers. Soc. Psych.*, **2** (1963): 20–29.

Lewin, K., *Field Theory in Social Science: Selected Theoretical Papers*, ed. Dorwin Cartwright, New York: Harper Torchbooks, 1951.

Linde, T. F., and C. H. Patterson, "Influence of orthopedic disability on conforming behavior," *J. Abnorm. Soc. Psych.*, **68** (1964): 115–118.

Lindskold, S., T. Bonoma, and J. T. Tedeschi, "Relative costs and reactions to threats," *Psychonomic Science*, **15** (1969): 205–207.

Luchins, A. S., and E. H. Luchins, "On conformity with true and false communications," *J. Soc. Psych.*, **42** (1955): 283–303.

Lumsdaine, A. A., and I. L. Janis, "Resistance to "counterpropaganda produced by one-sided and two-sided 'propaganda' presentations," *Pub. Opin. Quart.* **17** (1953): 311–318.

McCarrey, M. W., L. T. Dayhaw, and G. P. Chagnon, "Attitude shift, approval need and extent of psychological differentiation," *J. Soc. Psych.*, **84** (1971): 141–149.

McConnel, T. R. Jr., "Suggestibility in children as a function of chronological age," *J. Abnorm. Soc. Psych.*, **67** (1963): 286–289.

McCroskey, J. C., "Scales for the measurement of ethos," *Speech Monographs*, **33** (1966): 65–72.

McCroskey, J. C., "The effects of evidence in persuasive communication," *Western Speech*, **31** (1967): 189–199.

McCroskey, J. C., "A summary of experimental research on the effects of evidence in persuasive communication," *Quart. J. Speech.*, **55** (1969): 169–176.

McCroskey, J. C., "The effects of evidence as an inhibitor of counterpersuasion," *Speech Monographs*, **37** (1970): 188–194.

McCroskey, J. C., and W. H. Combs, "The effects of the use of analogy on attitude change and source credibility," *J. of Communication*, **19** (1969): 333–339.

McCroskey, J. C., and R. S. Mehrley, "The effects of disorganization and nonfluency on attitude change and source credibility," *Speech Monographs*, **36** (1969): 13–21.

McDavid, J. W., "Personality and situational determinants of conformity," *J. Abnorm. Soc. Psych.*, **58** (1959): 241–246.

McEwen, W., and B. Greenberg, "The effects of message intensity on receiver evaluations of source, message, and topic," *J. of Communication*, 20 (1970): 340–350.

McGinnies, E., "Studies in persuasion: III Reactions of Japanese students to one-sided and two-sided communications," *J. Soc. Psych.*, 70 (1966): 87–93.

McGuire, W. J., "Direct and indirect effects of dissonance-producing messages," *J. Abnorm. Soc. Psych*, 60 (1960): 354–358. (a)

McGuire, W. J., "Cognitive consistency and attitude change," *J. Abnorm. Soc. Psych.*, 60 (1960): 345–353. (b)

McGuire, W. J., "The effectiveness of supportive and refutational defenses in immunizing and restoring beliefs against persuasion," *Sociometry*, 24 (1961): 184–197.

McGuire, W. J., "Persistance of the resistance to persuasion induced by various types of prior belief defenses," *J. Abnorm. Soc. Psych.*, 64 (1962): 241–248.

McGuire, W. J., "Inducing resistance to persuasion," in L. Berkowitz, ed., *Advances In Experimental Social Psychology*, Vol. 1., New York: Academic Press, 1964, pp. 191–229.

McGuire, W. J., "Personality and susceptibility to social influence," in E. F. Burgather and W. W. Lambert, eds., *Handbook of Personality Theory and Research*, Chicago: Rand McNally, 1968, pp. 1130–1187.

McGuire, W. J., "The nature of attitudes and attitude change," in G. Lindzey and E. Aronson, eds., *The Handbook of Social Psychology*, 2d ed., Reading, Mass: Addison-Wesley, 1969, 136–314.

McGuire, W. J., and D. Papageargis, "The relative efficacy of various types of prior belief-defense in producing immunity to persuasion," *J. Abnorm. Soc. Psych.*, 62 (1961): 327–337.

McGurrin, M. C., "Person perception, dissonance, and resistance to persuasion," Ph.D. diss.: Temple University; Ann Arbor, Michigan: Xerox University Microfilms, No. 72–17, 703, 1972.

March, J., "An introduction to the theory and measurement of influence," *American Political Science Review*, 49 (1955): 431–451.

March, J., "Influence measurement in experimental and semi-experimental groups," *Sociometry*, 19 (1956): 260–271.

Maslow, A. H., *Motivation and Personality*, New York: Harper & Row, 1954.

Mausner, B., "The effect of one partner's success in a relevant task on the interaction of observer pairs," *J. Abnorm. Soc. Psych.*, 49 (1954): 557–560.

Menzel, H., "Public and private conformity under different conditions of acceptance in the group," *J. Abnorm. Soc. Psych.*, **55** (1957): 398–402.

Meunier, C., and B. G. Rule, "Anxiety, confidence, and conformity," *J. Pers.* **35** (1967): 498–504.

Miller, G. R., *Speech Communication: A Behavioral Approach*, Indianapolis: Bobbs-Merrill, 1966.

Miller, G. R., and J. Baseheart, "Source trustworthiness, opinionated statements, and response to persuasive communication," *Speech Monographs*, **36** (1969): 1–7.

Miller, G. R., and M. A. Hewgill, "The effects of variations in nonfluency on audience ratings of source credibility," *Quart. J. Speech*, **50** (1964): 36–44.

Miller, G. R., and M. A. Hewgill, "Some recent research on fear-arousing message appeals," *Speech Monographs*, **33** (1966): 377–391.

Miller, G. R., and J. Lobe, "Opinionated language, open and close-mindedness, and response to persuasive communications," *J. of Communication*, **27** (1967): 333–341.

Miller, G. R., and M. Rokeach, "Individual differences and tolerance for inconsistency," in Abelson, *et al.*, *Theories of Cognitive Consistency: A Sourcebook*, Chicago: Rand McNally, 1968, pp. 624–632.

Mills, J., "Opinion change as a function of the communicator's desire to influence and liking for the audience," *J. Exper. Soc. Psych.*, **2** (1966): 152–159.

Mills, J., and J. Harvey, "Opinion change as a function of when information about the communicator is received and whether he is attractive or expert," *J. Pers. Soc. Psych.*, **21** (1972): 52–55.

Mills, J., and Jellison, J. M., "Effect on opinion change of similarity between the communicator and the audience he addressed," *J. Pers. Soc. Psych.*, **9** (1968): 153–156.

Mischel, W., "Preference for delayed reinforcement and social responsibility," *J. Abnorm. Soc. Psych.*, **62** (1961): 1–7.

Moore, J. C., Jr., "Social studies of social influence: Process considerations," *Sociometry*, **32** (1969): 145–157.

Moore, R. K., "Susceptibility to hypnosis and susceptibility to social influence," *J. Abnorm. Soc. Psych.*, **68** (1964): 282–294.

Mortensen, C. D., *Communication: The Study of Human Interaction*, New York: McGraw-Hill, 1972.

Mulder, M. H., H. Mauk, and H. Wilke, "Participation and power equalization," *Organizational Behavior and Human Performance,* 5 (1970): 430–448.

Nadler, E. B., "Yielding, authoritarianism, and authoritarian ideology regarding groups," *J. Abnorm. Soc. Psych.,* 58 (1959): 408–410.

Newcomb, T. M., "An approach to the study of communicative acts," *Psych. Rev.,* 60 (1953): 393–404.

Newcomb, T. M., "The prediction of interpersonal attraction," *American Psychologist,* 11 (1956): 575–586.

New York Times, "37 who saw murder didn't call the police," March 27, 1964, p. 1.

Nicholas, K. B., R. E. McCarter, and R. V. Heckel, "The effects of race and sex on the imitation of television models," *J. Soc. Psych.,* 85 (1971): 315–316.

Nord, W., "Social exchange theory: An integrative approach to social conformity," *Psych. Bull.,* 71 (1969): 174–208.

Osgood, C. E., and P. H. Tannenbaum, "The principle of congruity in the prediction of attitude change," *Psych. Rev.,* 62 (1955): 42–55.

Ostermeier, T. H., "Effects of type and frequency of reference upon perceived source credibility and attitude change," *Speech Monographs,* 34 (1967): 137–144.

Pallak, M. S., and T. S. Pittman, "General motivational effects of dissonance arousal," *J. Pers. Soc. Psych.,* 21 (1972): 349–358.

Parsons, T., "On the concept of influence," *Pub. Opin. Quart.,* 27 (1963): 37–62.

Patel, A. A., and J. E. Gordon, "Some personal and situational determinants of yielding to influence," *J. Abnorm. Soc. Psych.,* 61 (1960): 411–418.

Pavlov, I. P., *Conditioned Reflexes,* London: Oxford Press, 1927.

Payne, W., "Negative labels: Passageways and prisons," *Crime and Delinquency,* 19 (1973): 33–40.

Pessin, J., and R. W. Husband, "Effects of social stimulation on human maze learning," *J. Abnorm. Soc. Psych.,* 28 (1933): 148–154.

Pollard, W. E., and T. R. Mitchell, "Decision theory analysis of social power," *Psych. Bull.,* 78 (1972): 433–446.

Powell, F. A., "Open and close-mindedness and the ability to differentiate source and message," *J. Abnorm. Soc. Psych.,* 65 (1962): 61.

Powell, F. A., and G. R. Miller, "Social approval and disapproval cues in anxiety-arousing communications," *Speech Monographs,* 34 (1967): 152–159.

Ray, M. L., "The effect of choice, controversy and selectivity on the effectiveness of various defenses to persuasion," Ph.D. diss., Northwestern University; Ann Arbor, Michigan: Xerox University Microfilms, No. 67–15, 322, 1967.

Rhine, R. J., and L. J. Severance, "Ego-involvement, discrepancy, source credibility, and attitude change," *J. Pers. Soc. Psych.*, **16** (1970): 175–190.

Riecken, H. W., "The effect of talkativeness on ability to influence group solutions of problems," *Sociometry*, **21** (1958): 309–321.

Rodman, G., "Effects of obscenity on source credibility and attitude change," unpublished M. S. thesis, Illinois State University, 1971.

Rosen, N. A., and R. S. Wyer, "Some further evidence for the 'Socratic Effect' using a subjective probability model of cognitive organization," *J. Pers. Soc. Psych.*, **24** (1972): 420–424.

Rosnow, R. L., and E. J. Robinson, eds., *Experiments In Persuasion*, New York: Academic Press, 1967.

Ross, A. S., and P. Wilson, "The effects of utility of information and intent on interpersonal esteem," *J. of Soc.Psych.*, **87** (1972): 83–88.

Rotter, J. B., "Generalized expectancies for internal versus external control of reinforcement," *Psych. Mono.*, **80** (1, whole no. 609), 1966.

Samelson, F., "Conforming behavior under two conditions of conflict in the cognitive field," *J. Abnorm. Soc. Psych.*, **55** (1957): 181–187.

Schacter, S., *The Psychology of Affiliation*, Stanford, Cal.: Stanford University Press, 1959.

Schachter, S., and J. E. Singer, "Cognitive, social and physiological determinants of emotional state," *Psych. Rev.*, **69** (1962): 379–399.

Schein, E. H., I. Schneier, and C. H. Barker, *Coercive Persuasion: A Socio-Psychological Analysis of the "Brainwashing" of American Civilian Prisoners by the Chinese Communists*, New York: Norton, 1961.

Schneider, F. W., "Conforming behavior of black and white children," *J. Pers. Soc. Psych.*, **16** (1970): 466–471.

Sears, D. O., "Opinion formation and information preferences in an adversary situation," *J. Exper. Soc. Psych.*, **2** (1966): 130–142.

Sereno, K. K., "Ego involvement, high source credibility, and response to a belief-discrepant communication," *Speech Monographs*, **35** (1968): 476–481.

Sereno, K. K., and E. M. Bodaken, "Ego-involvement and attitude change: Toward a reconceptualization of persuasive effect," *Speech Monographs*, 39 (1972): 151–158.

Sereno, K. K., and G. Hawkins, "The effects of variations in speaker's nonfluency upon the audience ratings of attitude toward the speech topic and speaker's credibility," *Speech Monographs*, 34 (1967): 58–64.

Sharp, H., and T. McClung, "Effects of organization on the speaker's ethos," *Speech Monographs*, 33 (1966): 182–183.

Shaw, M. E., *Group Dynamics: The Psychology of Small Group Behavior*, New York: McGraw-Hill, 1971.

Shaw, M. E., and P. Costanzo, *Theories of Social Psychology*, New York: McGraw-Hill, 1970.

Shor, R. E., "Shared patterns of nonverbal normative expectations in automobile driving," in L. Bickman and T. Henchy, eds., *Beyond the Laboratory: Field Research in Social Psychology*, New York: McGraw-Hill, 1972, pp. 319–323.

Siegel, E. R., G. R. Miller, and C. E. Wotring, "Source credibility and credibility proneness: A new relationship," *Speech Monographs*, 36 (1969): 118–125.

Sigall, H., and R. Helmreich, "Opinion change as function of stress and communicator credibility," *J. Exp. Soc. Psych.*, 5 (1969): 70–78.

Silverman, I., "On the resolution and tolerance of cognitive inconsistency in a natural-occurring event: Attitudes and beliefs following the Senator Edward M. Kennedy incident," *J. Pers. Soc. Psych.*, 17 (1971): 171–178.

Simmel, E. C., R. A. Hoppe, and G. A. Milton, eds. *Social Facilitation and Imitative Behavior*, Boston: Allyn and Bacon, 1968.

Sistrunk, F., "Negro-White comparisons in social conformity," *J. Soc. Psych.*, 85 (1971): 77–85.

Sistrunk, F., and J. McDavid, "Sex variable in conforming behavior," *J. Pers. Soc. Psych.*, 17 (1971): 200–207.

Smith, R. E., and F. Flenning, "Need for approval and susceptibility to unintended social influence," *J. of Consulting and Clinical Psych.*, 36 (1971): 383–385.

Snyder, A., W. Mischel, and B. E. Lott, "Value, information, and conformity behavior," *J. Pers.*, 28 (1960): 333–341.

Snyder, M., and M. Rothbart, "Communicator attractiveness and opinion change," *Canadian J. of Behavioral Sci.*, 3 (1971): 377–387.

Staats, A. W., K. A. Minke, C. H. Martin, and W. R. Higa, "Deprivation-satiation and strength of attitude conditioning: A test of attitude-reinforcer-discriminative theory," *J. Pers. Soc. Psych.*, 24 (1972): 178–185.

Staats, A. W., and C. K. Staats, "Attitudes established by classical conditioning," *J. Abnorm. Soc. Psych.*, 57 (1958): 37–40.

Steiner, I. D., and H. H. Johnson, "Authoritarianism and 'tolerance of trait inconsistency,' " *J. Abnorm. Soc. Psych.*, 67 (1963): 338–391.

Steiner, I. D., and J. S. Vannoy, "Personality correlates of two types of conformity behavior," *J. Pers. Soc. Psych.*, 4 (1966): 307–315.

Stotland, E., and L. K. Canon, *Social Psychology: A Cognitive Approach*, Philadelphia: Saunders, 1972.

Stuart, A., and J. M. Dabbs, "Physical distance and persuasion," *J. Pers. Soc. Psych.*, 15 (1970): 265–270.

Suppes, P., and F. Krasne, "Application of stimulus sampling theory to situations involving social pressure," *Psych. Rev.*, 68 (1961): 46–49.

Sutton-Smith, B., and B. G. Rosenberg, "Sibling consensus on power tactics," *J. of Genetic Psych.*, 112 (1968): 63–72.

Swenson, C., *Introduction to Interpersonal Relations*, Glenview, Illinois: Scott, Foresman, 1973.

Swingle, P. ed., *The Structure of Conflict*, New York: Academic Press, 1970.

Tedeschi, J. T., ed., *The Social Influence Processes*, Chicago: Aldine Atherton Press, 1972.

Tedeschi, J. T., "Threats and promises," in P. Swingle, ed., *The Structure of Conflict*, New York: Academic Press, 1970, pp. 155–192.

Thelen, M. H., "The effect of subject race, model race, and vicarious praise on vicarious learning," *Child Development*, 42 (1971): 972–977.

Thibaut, J. W., and L. H. Strickland, "Psychological set and social conformity," *J. Pers.*, 25 (1956): 115–129.

Thibaut, J. W., and H. H. Kelley, *The Social Psychology of Groups*, New York: John Wiley, 1959.

Torrance, E. P., "Some consequences of power differences on decision-making in permanent and temporary three-man groups," in A. P. Hare, E. F. Borgatta, and R. F. Bales, eds., *Small Groups*, New York: Knopf, 1965, pp. 600–609.

Triandis, H. C., *Attitude and Attitude Change*, New York: John Wiley, 1971.

Triplett, N., "The dynamogenic factors in pacemaking and competition," *Amer. J. of Psych.*, **9** (1897): 507–533.

Tubbs, S. L., "Explicit versus implicit conclusions and audience commitment," *Speech Monographs*, **35** (1968): 14–19.

Valins, S., "Cognitive effects of false heart-rate feedback," *J. Pers. Soc. Psych.*, **4** (1966): 400–408.

Vernon, M. D., ed., *Experiments In Visual Perception*, Baltimore: Penguin Books, 1966.

Walker, E. L., and R. W. Heyns, *An Anatomy for Conformity*, Belmont, Calif.: Brooks/Cole, 1962.

Walter, B., *Bureaucratic Communications: A Statistical Analysis of Influence*, Chapel Hill: University of North Carolina Press, 1963.

Walters, R. H., and P. Karal, "Social deprivation and verbal behavior," *J. Pers.*, **28** (1960): 89–107.

Walters, R. H., R. D. Parke, and V. A. Cane, "Timing of punishment and the observation of consequences to others as determinants of response inhibition," *J. Exp. Child Psych.*, **2** (1965): 10–30.

Warren, I. D., "The effect of credibility in sources of testimony on audience attitudes towards speaker and message," *Speech Monographs*, **36** (1969): 456–458.

Watzlawick, P., J. Beavin, and D. Jackson, *Pragmatics of Human Communication, A Study of Interactional Patterns, Pathologies, and Paradoxes*, New York: Norton, 1967.

Weiss, R. F., "An extension of Hullian learning theory to persuasive communication," in A. G. Greenwald, T. C. Brock, and T. N. Ostrom, eds., *Psychological Foundations of Attitudes*, New York: Academic Press, 1968, pp. 109–146.

Weiss, W., "Opinion congruence with a negative source on one issue as a factor influencing agreement on another issue," *J. Abnorm. Soc. Psych.*, **54** (1957): 180–186.

Wenburg, J. R., "The relationships among audience adaptation, source credibility, and types of message cues," Ph.D. diss., Michigan State University, 1969.

Wenburg, J., and W. Wilmot, *The Personal Communication Process*, New York: John Wiley, 1973.

Wheeler, L., "Toward a theory of behavioral contagion," *Psych. Rev.*, **73** (1966): 179–192.

Wheeler, L., *Interpersonal Influence*, Boston: Allyn and Bacon, 1970.

Williams, J. E., R. D. Tucker, and F. Y. Dunham, "Changes in the connotations of color names among Negroes and Caucasians," *J. Pers. Soc. Psych.*, **19** (1971): 222–228.

Willis, R. H., "Two dimensions of conformity-non-conformity," *Sociometry*, **26** (1963): 499–513.

Wyer, R. S., Jr., "Behavioral correlates of academic achievement: conformity under achievement-and affiliation-incentive conditions," *J. Pers. Soc. Psych.*, **6** (1967): 255–263.

Zajonc, R. B., "Social facilitation," *Science*, **149** (1965): 269–274.

Zajonc, R. B., "The attitudinal effects of mere exposure," *J. Pers. Soc. Psych., Monograph Supplement*, **9** (1968): 1–27.

Zajonc, R. B., and J. Morrissetti, "The role of uncertainty in cognitive change," *J. Abnorm. Soc. Psych.*, **61** (1960): 168–175.

Zajonc, R. B., and S. M. Sales, "Social facilitation of dominant and subordinate responses," *J. Exper. Soc. Psych.*, **2** (1966): 160–168.

Zajonc, R. B., R. J. Wolosin, M. A. Wolosin, and W. D. Loh, "Social facilitation and imitation in group risk-taking," *J. Exp. Soc. Psych.*, **6** (1970): 26–46.

Zillmann, D. "Rhetorical elicitation of agreement in persuasion, *J. Pers. Soc. Psych.*, **21** (1972): 159–165.

Zimbardo, P. G., "Involvement and communication discrepancy as determinants of opinion conformity," *J. Abnorm. Soc. Psych.*, **60** (1960): 86–94.

Zipf, S., "Resistance and conformity under reward and punishment," *J. Abnorm. Soc. Psych.*, **61** (1960): 102–109.

Author Index

Subject Index